For Grace

THE TALE
OF ALICE'S QUILT

JENNIFER BLOMGREN

with kindest regards,

Jennifer
Blomgren

Martingale®
& COMPANY

The Tale of Alice's Quilt
© 2008 by Jennifer Blomgren

Martingale®
& COMPANY

That
Patchwork
Place®

That Patchwork Place® is an imprint of Martingale & Company®.

Martingale & Company
20205 144th Ave. NE
Woodinville, WA 98072-8478 USA
www.martingale-pub.com

CREDITS

President & CEO: *Tom Wierzbicki*
Publisher: *Jane Hamada*
Editorial Director: *Mary V. Green*
Managing Editor: *Tina Cook*
Contributing Editor: *Virginia Lauth*
Technical Editor: *Robin Strobel*
Copy Editor: *Melissa Bryan*
Design Director: *Stan Green*
Assistant Design Director: *Regina Girard*
Story Illustrator: *Jennifer Blomgren*
Technical Illustrator: *Adrienne Smitke*
Cover Designer: *Stan Green*
Text Designer: *Trina Craig*
Photographer: *Brent Kane*

Printed in China
13 12 11 10 09 08   8 7 6 5 4 3 2 1

Library of Congress Cataloging-in-Publication Data
Library of Congress Control Number: 2007041243

ISBN: 978-1-56477-833-8

MISSION STATEMENT
Dedicated to providing quality products and service to inspire creativity.

DEDICATION

To my sisters, Brenda and Jo Ann

ACKNOWLEDGMENTS

I WOULD LIKE TO ACKNOWLEDGE my family for their tremendous support of my efforts in writing and illustration, starting in early childhood and continuing to this day, and for the sense of history and continuity they have given me as well. They have all helped me immeasurably—both materially and intangibly—with their hard work on my behalf and their loving encouragement, and I am grateful beyond words.

I owe a special debt to Eileen Garling, the "Goddess of Quilting," who, beginning in my college years, fed the fires of my interest in quilting. Her impeccable technique and her generosity in sharing her knowledge have been invaluable on many levels. She was a true artist, and her beautiful quilts will live on just as she herself, though gone now, will live in many hearts.

I also wish to thank the members of my Wednesday Night Writers group, Dahti Blanchard (who began the group), Kate Snow, Libby Urner, Karen Frank, Jolie Stekly, and honorary member Marion Bartl for their endless patience, constructive critiques, and unflagging support. They gave me the final nudge I needed to tell this story.

CONTENTS

CHAPTER ONE

ALICE JUNE WOKE UP just as her mother was reaching to pull the chain and turn off the girl's reading light. She had tiptoed in so quietly, she almost got away with it. But Alice June smiled sleepily and said, "Don't turn it off . . . I haven't finished the chapter. I have to see what happens."

"No, you don't," said Momma. "It'll be the same chapter tomorrow and you can see then."

"Wait—don't go yet. I wanted to ask you something today and forgot."

"Well, what is it? I don't want you to get all the way waked up. You have school tomorrow."

"You know that old quilt in the cedar chest? The one I saw when you got out the wool hats? I saw a sign at the fairgrounds about a quilt show. Is that for quilts like ours?"

Momma cocked her head, thinking. "I can't say I know for sure. The quilters' club must be putting it on. But I would guess it would have some old-fashioned quilts, kind of like the one we have."

"Could we go see?" Alice June asked.

"If you go to sleep now," Momma said and laughed.

"OK, but first, tell me—where did our quilt come from?"

"That's a long story . . . one for tomorrow!" And she backed out of the room, her finger to her lips, leaving Alice June to lie awake, wondering. But not for long; soon, she slept.

IN THE CAR on the way home from school the next day, Alice June reminded Momma of her promise to tell the story.

"I'm not sure where to begin; how many years ago, that is."

"What do you mean?"

"Well, it really all began when people started quilting. I think that was in China thousands of years ago."

"You don't have to go back that far!" exclaimed Alice June.

"OK, then, I'll start in 1864. That was when your dad's family moved out West to Oregon. Remember I told you they were pioneers?"

"Sort of. But how were they pioneers?"

"Did you ever learn about the Oregon Trail?"

"They had a special about it on TV and I saw the first part but you made me go to bed."

"Well, maybe I should have let you stay up that night," Momma said. "After all, it is your heritage."

"My what?" Alice June asked.

"Your heritage," Momma said, "is your history. It's what you inherited, in a way, from your family. Not just money, or things like that, but what they did, and how that has helped to make you who you are now. It's hard to explain exactly. For instance, your great-great-grandmother walked 2,000 miles out West on the Oregon Trail when she was just eight years old. Just three years younger than you! And her name was Alice, too. That's who you are named for."

"Really? She had my name?"

"Well, not exactly. Her name was Alice Jane, and—as you know, of course—we named you Alice June. The June is after my mother. But the name Alice came down through five generations, beginning with that little girl in the covered wagon. That's part of your heritage."

"Did she make the quilt? In a real covered wagon?"

"No, her granddaughter did, much, much later, on their farm in Oregon. In a covered wagon, you can't really quilt that much, not usually. They walked all day, just about every day until it was nearly dark, and then they had to make camp and cook and take care of their oxen."

"What are oxen?"

"Kind of like big, strong cows."

"Why did they walk all day? Why didn't they ride in the wagon?"

"They did sometimes, I guess, if they were sick or too tired or too little. But they walked all they could to make it easier on the oxen. After all, they had to pull a long way."

"How long did it take to get to Oregon?"

Momma thought for a minute. "Well, it seems I remember your dad saying they left in April from Missouri, and they got there in early November. I think he said Alice Jane had her ninth birthday along the way somewhere."

Alice June sat back, wondering, trying to imagine. From earliest spring, when the trees were just budding and the delicate smells of fresh grass and rain were so sweet, to old November when the leaves were long dead and on the ground, and it was dark so early at night—walking all day, every day!

"But," Momma said, interrupting her thoughts, "we're talking about the quilt. The Oregon Trail is a long story of its own! But it does figure in the story of the quilt, because if the family hadn't come out West, everything would have been different and probably your great-aunt, who made the quilt, wouldn't have been born."

This last comment was a little confusing, but Alice June was too busy thinking to bother asking her mother to explain. She was thinking about the quilt. It was soft, and worn, and much of the color was faded. But there were some squares of a beautiful blue. The printed patches looked so old-fashioned and there were funny stitches all over it. It even smelled old, like dust and cedar and old dried flowers.

"What was her name? The one who made the quilt?"

Momma turned to her and smiled.

"Alice," she said, "Alice Patricia. Like I said, she was your great-aunt. She had some trouble with her heart—something that doctors would have a much better chance of fixing these days—and she couldn't run and play like the other kids. So she became a quilter, and a very good one."

"How come I never knew about her? Did she live to be old?" Alice June asked.

"No," Momma said gently. "She was only 12 when she died. But she left a lot to remember her by. Did you know about those squares waiting to be sewn together to make the top of a quilt?"

"Where are they? What do they look like?"

"Over at Aunt Joy's house, I think," said Momma. "Do you still want to go to the quilt show?"

"Yes, and to Aunt Joy's, too. We could take Aunt Joy with us to the show."

"Good idea." Momma smiled and looked over at her daughter. But Alice June was lost in thought, wondering about this little girl, whose name she had, and whom she had never met.

CHAPTER TWO

*I*T WAS A CLEAR, still, warm fall afternoon when they pulled into the fairgrounds for the quilt show. The sunlight had that soft feel as it washed its gold over the big-leaf maple trees standing here and there, shouting a brilliant yellow, in the pastures surrounding the buildings. They seemed almost like torches against the bright solid blue of the Indian summer sky.

It was so quiet, too; you could hear an occasional car door slam, the distant laughing of a few friends walking to and from the parking lot, a single dog barking across the valley. But there was a hush that lay over this September day, especially in the hall where the quilts hung.

There were dozens of them, draping full length from wooden rods, displayed back to back in groups of three so that they made little open rooms all the way down both sides of the long room. Each one was completely different from all the others and they had magical names like Eight Hands Round, Tumbling Blocks, Tall Pine Tree, Jacob's Ladder, Texas Star, Eternal Triangle. Some were made of crazily patched, deeply colored velvets, embroidered in exotic stitches; some were of pale cottons, floating almost like dreams, waving gently at a light touch.

They walked slowly—Aunt Joy, Alice June, and her mother—past quilts pieced of triangles, squares, and circles. Some had designs of flowers, trees, vines, and leaves cut of fabric and carefully stitched by hand on top of snow-white cloth. All had tiny stitches covering nearly every inch of their surface.

In a corner sat a very small old lady, and at her feet was an enormous basket overflowing with a large quilt. She was stitching within a circle of wood that held a section of the quilt, drawn tight. Along the edges of the quilt were birds and leaves, delicately stitched.

Aunt Joy touched Alice June on the shoulder and whispered, "My neighbor is in the quilt club. She told me about this lady, Mrs. Pearl. They say she is a real artist."

Alice June watched this tiny lady who had created such a beautiful thing, so much bigger than she was, and thought of her great-aunt, who never lived beyond childhood. She must have sat sewing just like this old lady, using the same kinds of things—a wooden frame, a needle and thread, and some scraps of fabric. Only, she had been on an Oregon homestead in a beautiful, lonely little valley far away in both time and distance. Then Alice June thought of something.

"Momma?"

"Yes?"

"If Alice Patricia, you know, the girl who made our quilt, had lived, how old would she be now?"

"Hmmmmm. Let me think. Probably about 80 or so. Your great-uncle Bobbie would know. He's the only one of the family still living who actually knew her. He's the youngest of the three kids, and he's about 78, as I remember."

"How old do you think this lady is?" Alice June asked.

"Well, that's hard to say. But I'd reckon her to be close to that—anywhere from mid 70s to mid 80s. Why?"

"I was just wondering." But Alice June was doing more than wondering. What if her great-aunt had lived? Would she be like this lady, one of the best quilters, admired by the others? What would she have looked like if she had lived to be old?

Alice June wondered whether anyone even remembered what she looked like, or if there were any photographs of her at all. Except for the quilts, she seemed to have vanished without a trace.

"Does Uncle Bobbie remember her?" Alice June asked of her mom.

"Well, he must have been about 10 when she died. Probably he remembers something."

Alice June looked up again at the long hall full of hard work, and at the lady named Mrs. Pearl, and again the image of a young girl in an old farmhouse came into her mind, piecing together scraps of old dresses. What did she think about, during all those quiet hours? And could Uncle Bobbie tell them anything more about her? A determination grew in Alice June to discover more.

CHAPTER THREE

ALICE JUNE WROTE in her most careful penmanship:

Dear Uncle Bobbie,

I just got back from Aunt Joy's house, where Momma and I looked at some quilt pieces that your sister Alice Patricia made. They are very pretty. There is a butterfly in every square and they are all so different. I'm having trouble telling you what they look like so here is a picture. They look like this, sort of.

These squares are just squares, they are not made into a quilt yet.

Momma told me you might remember Alice Patricia. Since we have the same first name I want to know about her. I hope you are fine. Please write.

Love,

Alice June

Alice June didn't know Uncle Bobbie very well; she had only seen him four or five times in her life, for visits of just a few days each time. Maybe that was why she didn't tell him that the name wasn't the only reason she wanted to know more about Alice Patricia.

He lived over in the Blue Mountains of Oregon, in the little town where he had grown up. He had come on the bus twice to see her family, and she and Dad had gone to meet him. He was not tall, but not short, a little stooped, but not very. He had broad shoulders and big hands, a weathered face, and gold teeth in the front. He had worked on the railroad and still wore, every day, the same kind of striped overalls he had worn for his job. He carried a leather suitcase when he traveled, and in it were history books for him to read, and candy for her, along with his shirts and overalls, of course.

She had been with her family to see him, two or three times, in his small white house down the hill from the homestead. Bobbie's family had moved to town, partly to be close to the doctor, just a year or two before Alice Patricia died. Just a few years after that, their mother had died, too. Dad had told her the homestead was sold a few years later, during the war, when Uncle Bobbie and his older brother were away in the army. When they came home, after the surrender, Bobbie moved into that same little house with his dad. His brother, who had married and started a family, went farther north and west, to be near his wife's people. That was Alice June's grandpa, Joe.

Uncle Bobbie's job with the trains took him away for weeks at a time, and he saw no sense, he said, in getting another house just to have it stand empty. And when he retired, after his dad had passed away, he came back and lived there alone.

It was hot there in the summer, and dry; enormous locust trees surrounded the place and dropped their olive-green leaves into the dust, and their roots had cracked the sidewalk all apart. The lawn was emerald, though, and lush, and Uncle Bobbie had tall rosebushes, heavily fragrant in the warm evenings. She remembered the constant loud song of the crickets at night, and how she had seen faraway lightning flash silently over the mountains from the back bedroom window. The whole little town and everything in it was so old, just like the house itself—old and clean and spare and quiet. Alice June felt, without knowing why, or how, the presence of the past and its people and memories so strongly that she could almost see and hear and smell them, but not quite. The old clock on the bookcase chimed every quarter hour and half hour, and on the hour it would bong out a short melody and then ten bongs for 10 o'clock, eleven for 11 o'clock, and so on. She would lie awake in the warm hush of the deep night, the only noise the crickets and the clock, and listen, counting. It seemed as though, even when the clock was ticking and bonging the hours and days away, that here, time stood still.

CHAPTER FOUR

*S*HE WAS LOOKING at the quilt in the cedar chest two weeks later when Momma called to her and said that a letter had come from Uncle Bobbie. Alice June lowered the heavy, fragrant lid and came running.

Dear Alice June,

I am glad you asked me about Alice Patricia. I do recall fairly well, though I was only 9 or 10 when she died. We shared the downstairs bedroom on the farm. She was quite sick as I remember. I never knew her to be able to run or play. She loved the outdoors, though, and whenever the weather allowed, she would do her sewing out on the porch or by the creek, usually with her dog, Stubby, close by. She read a lot, too, especially poems, and sometimes she wrote them.

I am sorry it took me so long to write back but I decided to send you a photograph of her and had to have another one made, as I had but one of that pose, and didn't want to give it up.

She was a little shy and didn't talk a lot, but did have a wonderful smile, as you will see. I hope you all are well.

With love from your Uncle Bobbie

ALICE JUNE UNFOLDED THE PAPER wrapped around a small, brown-toned photograph of a girl about her age, with dark eyes and heavy eyebrows, and a heart-shaped face. She had light brown hair cut like Peter Pan's, and a wide grin beneath a turned-up nose. She looked tired, but Alice June was drawn to a certain look in her eyes. They were full of life, somehow, though there were shadows beneath them. She wore a calico dress, with tucks and small ruffles and a bow at the dropped waist, and stood on the front porch of a white farmhouse, next to a porch swing.

Alice June showed the picture to her mother. "Who does she look like?"

Momma looked, smiled, and looked again. "I think she looks a little like you." And it was true. She did. It was the smile.

ALICE JUNE BOUGHT A SMALL GOLD FRAME for the picture and put it on her dresser, and she wrote to Uncle Bobbie to thank him. She wanted to tell him something, but didn't know how. She wanted to say that she felt she knew Alice Patricia, too; but it sounded too silly to say that she felt she knew her from her quilts. But it was true, just like the resemblance was true.

CHAPTER FIVE

*C*HRISTMASTIME CAME, with its fresh woodsy smells from the tree, its shivers of delight and anticipation, brightly wrapped packages hidden in unexpected places, and the warm buttery scent of cookies baking. Christmas brought with it the tradition in Alice June's family of knocking on the close neighbors' doors, carrying gifts of homemade divinity and fudge, and singing a carol for them when they opened the door. With Christmas, too, came a gift from Uncle Bobbie, wrapped in white tissue and tied with a blue ribbon. It was in addition to his usual tin of peppermint candy for the family and a five-dollar bill for her. Early on that wet, dark, blustery Christmas morning, she folded back the snowy white tissue paper and found a small scrapbook, light gray, held together with faded black cord, the tassels tattered and a little dusty. In it were pasted newspaper clippings, a program from a sixth-grade graduation ceremony dated May 25, 1929, and a few small sheets of paper written carefully in a childish hand. His accompanying letter said:

> *Dear Alice June,*
>
> *I found this old album in the back of the closet upstairs. I looked it over again and copied the verses, and decided that you should have it, since you wondered about your great-aunt Alice Patricia. This will tell you more about her, since she wrote the poems, including the one published in the local paper. I hope you like it and I know you will take good care of it, because it is really one of the few treasures left of my sister.*
>
> *With affection,*
>
> *Your Uncle Bobbie*

Without thinking, Alice June hugged the little book closely. He had said it was one of the few treasures left of his sister. And he had given it to her. For a moment, she stood quietly, taking it all in. She turned to look at her mother, who was watching her intently. "Momma, I can't believe he gave this to me. Here, read the letter." Her mother read it, shook her head slightly, and handed it back to Alice June.

"You'll want to take good care of it," she said, "and I know you will."

Alice June kept the scrapbook in the top drawer of her dresser, under the photo of Alice Patricia, and would reread the poems now and then. She developed a favorite, which went like this:

I sit by the hour, shaded from the sun
Saying very little to anyone
The tree branches whisper, as I quietly stitch
My little dog stops to scratch an itch;
We sit there together, friends always
And while away the hours of the long summer days.

CHAPTER SIX

*S*CHOOL STARTED AGAIN, and the winds of January were cold and harsh. As the short overcast days went by, Alice June was busy. She had ballet every Wednesday and piano lessons on Thursdays and there was school, of course, and homework and her chores and her best friend, Lindsay. They took turns staying at each other's houses on Friday nights and sometimes Saturdays, too. Alice June had several friends she would sometimes ride bikes with, or go to the movies with, but Lindsay was the one she felt closest to. She could tell her just about anything.

She liked going to Lindsay's house because it was so full of life and commotion. Three mischievous little brothers, two playful terriers, a lizard, a cat, and four parrots kept the place cheerful, noisy, and far from dull, especially the time when little Ben's iguana, Darwin, got out and nobody could find him for days. Finally Lindsay's grandma discovered him sleeping beneath a huge pile of clean laundry.

"And," Lindsay said, "you could hear her scream all the way to the corner."

LINDSAY'S MOTHER WORKED as a waitress and put dinner on the table with a no-nonsense air, slapping down plates, snapping her gum, and serving up huge portions of Alice June's favorites: macaroni and cheese or scalloped potatoes or homemade spaghetti. Then they'd watch a video and after that crawl into Lindsay's bed under the eaves and talk while the rain pattered on the roof. One night they started talking about Alice Patricia.

"How did you find out about her?" Lindsay asked.

"I asked Momma about the quilt in our old trunk. Alice Patricia made that and the quilt squares too."

"What squares?"

"My Aunt Joy has them at her house. There are 20 of them, each with a different butterfly out of scraps of fabric. She embroidered the antennae and the bodies. They're really good."

"In that picture you have she looks sort of our age. How did she learn to do all that?"

"Momma said the older ladies taught all the girls to sew. Everybody did it, the women, I mean. But she spent lots and lots of time at it because she was too sick to do anything else. There was something wrong with her heart."

"She couldn't do anything else?" Lindsay asked, startled.

"Well, I guess not much else," answered Alice June. "She read, and wrote a little poetry, and stayed quiet mostly."

Lindsay was quiet, absorbing the idea of being 12 years old and unable to do more than remain quiet and read and sew. After a while she gave up trying to imagine it and began to get very sleepy. But she just had to ask one more question.

"Alice June?"

"Hmmmmm?"

"Do the butterflies look like they're playing? On the squares, I mean."

"Yes," murmured Alice June, very drowsily. "They're dancing."

AT ABOUT THIS TIME, in January, little packages and notes began arriving from Uncle Bobbie every few days. Alice June would come home from school to find something addressed to her, in his handwriting, propped up on the kitchen table against the sugar bowl.

He was starting to "go through some boxes in the attic," he said in the first letter, and had found a few little things that "had had something to do with your great-aunt Alice Patricia." Once, it was a small oval locket of silver, engraved with leaves and flowers. In it was a tiny, crudely cut, slightly blurred photograph of Stubby. The next thing was a wide, sky-blue hair ribbon, soft and satiny, grown fragile with age, still wrinkled where the bow had been tied. Another envelope held a snapshot of two serious little boys and a dark-haired girl with a gentle smile, lying on the ground, peeping out from beneath a blanket hung over a clothesline. There was a hand-printed program for a play with Bobbie as "The Servant Boy," Alice Patricia as "The Garden Princess," and Joe as "A Knight from Afar." A child-sized bracelet, made from rolled-paper beads of blue and yellow and coated with shellac, arrived in a little white box, and then came a pair of small hand-crocheted white cotton gloves, a little yellowed now, obviously Sunday best. Then, as Groundhog Day approached, Alice June opened a letter to find a poem in a child's writing, entitled "Stubby's Progress," only the "Progress" was spelled "Porgress." It was two pages long and funny as it told of how Alice Patricia's mother tried to make the dog live on the back porch but soon he was in the kitchen, then in the parlor, then gradually he had worked his way to sleeping by the stove and finally in Alice Patricia's bed.

Sometimes Uncle Bobbie wrote a little note to go along with the keepsake and sometimes he didn't. Alice June replied to everything he sent with a thank-you, but it never seemed like enough. After all, these were pieces of his sister, pieces of his memories. Through these tiny things she could guess her great-aunt's favorite color, could learn about her sense of fun, her imagination, her love for her dog and for her brothers. She could imagine her in church next to Uncle Bobbie, wearing the lacy gloves, and see her dressed in grown-up clothes as the "Garden Princess." These things smelled old and musty but there was a young freshness about them, too.

It felt like he was sending her freeze-frames of another world, long ago and far away, and indeed, he was. Yet, it was oddly familiar to her, and receiving these precious things made her feel honored and grateful and sad and comforted, all at the same time.

She carefully put each one away in her drawer beneath the framed picture, and each time she looked at them, she wished she knew more about the girl they had belonged to.

Chapter Seven

IN EARLY FEBRUARY, Alice June's dad said he was going on a business trip the next week and asked her if she would mind if he took Momma along.

"You could stay with Aunt Joy," he said, "What do you think?"

Alice June nodded her agreement with the plan. She would miss them, and home, but it was only for four days. And, she had a question for Aunt Joy.

"Could I look at those quilt squares again?" she asked, as soon as she had put her duffel bag and backpack in the spare room.

"Sure," Aunt Joy said. "They're right where we left them, in the linen closet upstairs."

"Can I lay them out on the bed in Janet's old room like we did before?"

"I don't see why not," Aunt Joy said. "Maybe I'll come see too after you're done spreading them out."

Alice June carefully took the soft squares of off-white muslin and laid them out.

"One, two, three, four across," she said out loud to herself, "and five down."

When Aunt Joy came in, Alice June asked her why the squares didn't look big enough to cover up a bed all the way.

"I think you're supposed to sew fabric between the squares, maybe of a different color, one that looks nice with the others. I think I remember Mrs. Lucchetti saying that's called the sashing."

"Mrs. Lucchetti?"

"Yes, my neighbor. She belongs to the quilters' club. Remember that very tiny old lady who does the beautiful quilts—the one in the corner at the show? Mrs. Lucchetti knows her. They quilt together on Monday afternoons, I think, over at the recreation center."

Alice June was listening, but she was looking, too, at those 20 butterflies fastened to the white background fabric with tiny, carefully taken stitches, bordered with curving lines and dots of colored embroidery thread. They were made of calico prints, but very different from what you would see now. They had odd little triangles, tiny cakes and bow ties, funny-looking flowers and polka dots, stripes, and even a plaid pattern. They looked so old-fashioned, in spite of the bright hues of gold, yellow, blue, red, peach, and green, a little dusty but only slightly faded. And each butterfly had a pair of antennae delicately sewn with black embroidery thread, whimsically curled about themselves.

"Can we leave it out for a day or two?" Alice June asked.

"Sure. Just keep the door shut. You know how Alfred likes to jump up on beds."

Alfred was a gray poufy cat who usually slept in the spare room. Finding Alice June there didn't stop him. He curled up on the pillow next to her head and by morning was sleeping on her face. She didn't mind, not even the snoring, which may have been loud purring. Now and then his kneading claws poked her a little, but mostly it was nice.

The next day, Friday, she rode to Aunt Joy's on the county bus when school was out, and coming into the kitchen found someone there she had never met before. She was older than Mom and Aunt Joy, with frizzy gray hair, but her eyes were twinkly and snappy. She wore funny tan stockings, old-fashioned clunky shoes, a white dress with blue polka dots, and a belt to match.

Aunt Joy stood up and said, "Alice June, I'd like you to meet Mrs. Lucchetti, my neighbor. She dropped by for a few minutes to catch me up on the news."

Alice June smiled and offered her hand to Mrs. Lucchetti, who shook it briskly and decisively.

"I hear you like quilts," Mrs. Lucchetti said. "So do I."

"Aunt Joy says you make them. Is it hard?"

"Well," Mrs. Lucchetti responded, tilting her head as she thought, "that's hard to say. It depends. Any way you look at it, it's work. There are a lot of tricks to learn. But it's fun, too, especially with a bunch of friends helping you."

"Has Mrs. Lucchetti seen the squares you have?" Alice June asked, turning to Aunt Joy.

"You have squares? And you didn't tell me?" Mrs. Lucchetti laughed.

"They've been in the family for years," Aunt Joy said. "I don't know exactly how I ended up with them. Alice June's folks have an old quilt from the same girl. That would be Joe's—Alice June's dad—and my aunt. You know I never liked to sew, any more than I like to cook and clean, but here they are. Good thing I'm such a pack rat, or they might have been lost. But these were in the family, after all, and they are very nice. Even I can tell that."

Alice June smiled to herself. Aunt Joy was fun, zany even, with her dyed red hair and loud voice and big pearl necklaces and corny jokes. Her daughter, Janet, had gone off to college and Aunt Joy had been divorced so long, Alice June didn't even remember her ex-husband's name. Aunt Joy always referred to him as "what's his name," anyway, though Momma said they were still friends and went out to lunch sometimes. She was tall and skinny and taught art to grade-school kids and drove an old turquoise Volvo covered with bumper stickers. She had big messy art projects everywhere in her cluttered house, from clay beads to oil paintings to papier-mâché piñatas for school parties. It was lots of fun there, but Aunt Joy wasn't very domestic. She changed Alfred's kitty litter now and then, but that was about all the housekeeping she went in for. Alice June usually ate pizza three times a day when she stayed there, but that was fine. She liked pizza, and she liked Aunt Joy.

Alice June asked, "Would you like to see the squares, Mrs. Lucchetti? Is that OK, Aunt Joy?"

"Sure. You lead the way."

"You bet your boots," said Mrs. Lucchetti.

Upstairs, Mrs. Lucchetti whistled a long, appreciative note when she saw the squares. "Who did you say did these?"

Aunt Joy spoke up. "Our dad's sister, Alice Patricia. I never knew her. She died very young from heart trouble, I think. She had to stay quiet a lot."

Alice June said, "She couldn't play with the other kids. And she wrote poetry, too."

"She did?" Aunt Joy asked, quite surprised. "You know," she said slowly, with a thoughtful look on her face, "she must have been something. I've never thought much about her until now. It's funny we don't know more about her."

"This is beautiful work, especially considering her age," Mrs. Lucchetti said. "A real heirloom. You'd better hang on to these, and keep them in the family."

"I've got half a mind to give them to Alice June's folks. I'll never do anything with them."

"Well, do as you please. But make sure somebody hangs on to them!"

Alice June knew the squares were a treasure, but as an idea grew swiftly in her mind, she was hoping to find a way to keep them in the family and share them, too.

BACK AT HOME, Alice June and her mother were folding clothes on the kitchen table when Alice June announced she wanted to learn how to make quilts.

"If I learn how, could I use the squares that Alice Patricia made and put them into a quilt?"

Momma turned, her arms loaded with clean towels, and looked at Alice June.

"Well, I'm not really the one to ask. Those came from your dad's side of the family. You'd better ask him and Aunt Joy. And, you know, I'm not able to help you much."

"I know. Aunt Joy isn't either. She already told me so. Neither one of you even likes to sew on buttons. I have an idea, though."

"What's your idea?"

"When I stayed with Aunt Joy, her neighbor Mrs. Lucchetti looked at the squares. She's a quilter and she even sews with that really little old lady we saw at the show last fall, the one who makes the fanciest quilts."

"Did she say she'd teach you?"

"No, I didn't ask her yet. But I want to join the quilters' club. She's in it. I want to learn from all of them."

"Is that possible? Do they take people as young as you are?"

"I don't know," said Alice June. "But why wouldn't they? Alice Patricia was quilting when she was my age."

Momma hugged her towels with one arm and squeezed Alice June's shoulder with the other.

"I'm sure you'll figure out a way if there is one."

Alice June went into action that very afternoon. She first asked her dad if she could use the squares his aunt had made. He said yes, if Aunt Joy approved. She then called Aunt Joy and left a message. Just before supper, Aunt Joy called back and said that it would please her very much to have them made into a quilt. "I'll never do anything with them!" she said repeatedly.

The next step was to write a letter to the quilters' club, which she would send in care of Aunt Joy.

The letter read:

Dear Mrs. Lucchetti (and the Quilters' Club),

My name is Alice June and we met at my Aunt Joy's house. You saw some quilt squares there that my great-aunt made a long time ago. I would like to make them into a quilt but I don't know how. I was wondering if I could come to the quilters' club and learn from you and the other quilters. I am 11 years old. I hope that is OK. Please write back and let me know. Thank you.

Sincerely,

Alice June

A WEEK WENT BY and it was a time of year when a week makes a big difference in the feel of the air and the look of the land. It was the earliest spring, with pussy willows, fuzzy pearl gray and delicate soft brown, appearing on bare branches, and the sun, though still pale and a little wan, shining with enough extra warmth that you could smell the earth, damp and loaded with life. Bulbs pushed up green tips an inch or two, nudging old dead leaves aside. In the afternoons the sky would clear its tattered clouds aside for sweet sunsets of rose pink and robin's-egg blue. Everything was washed with fresh rain at least once a day and the grass was wet and sparkled in the sun. It was the very beginning of the long, damp, cool spring that Alice June so loved. This was her favorite time of year, so full of promise and so new.

Finally, on a Tuesday after school, the phone rang and it was Aunt Joy.

"I have a message for you from Mrs. Lucchetti. She had to talk to the members about your request at their weekly meeting, and that's why it took this long to get an answer."

Alice June's heart jumped and the phone shook a little in her hand. "Well? What did she say?"

Aunt Joy cleared her throat to announce: "I have a one-sentence message and it says: 'Be there 3:00 p.m. Monday, bring squares, and welcome to the youngest-ever member of the Log Cabin Quilters' Club.'"

Alice June was surprised to find she was crying. For a moment she couldn't talk. Then, her practical side rose to the occasion.

"Where do they meet?"

"At the recreation center uptown. Go around the building to Taylor Street. There's an outside door to a daylight basement, across from the old Methodist Church. They're down there. Just knock loudly."

She thanked Aunt Joy and hung up, grinning. She was forming a plan. "I'll ask Mom for permission to take the uptown bus and to pick me up afterward. And I'll take the squares to school in my backpack and not let go of it all day."

Alice June didn't realize it then, but she was about to start, in this season of renewal, not just a quilt, but a new chapter that would change her life.

CHAPTER EIGHT

ALICE JUNE KEPT HER BACKPACK close to her all day on Monday. When she sat at her desk, and at lunch, she looped the straps around her leg, and held it next to her body everywhere she went. That morning she had taken the squares from the cedar chest where they'd been since Aunt Joy brought them over, carefully wrapped them in tissue paper, then in a plastic bag, folded the bag into quarters, and placed it carefully in the zipper pocket in the back of her pack. All day she was aware of them.

When the last bell rang at 2:30 she walked quickly to the bus stop, just a block from school, on the main street of town. She saw the sign "Uptown District" above the windshield of the approaching bus, and when it stopped with a squeal and the doors opened with a hiss, she watched two old ladies and a young man with a bicycle helmet get off. The young man unfastened his bike and rode away. The driver called, "Anyone for uptown?" Alice June strode to the door, grabbed the rail, and climbed on, tinkling 50 cents into the holder. The driver tipped his hat and smiled, and as soon as she sat down, he shifted the gears and off they went. The bus rumbled through the older part of town where people were restoring houses built in the days of the sailing ships, past the big park that stood on the bluff leading down to the beach, and around the corner to the little shopping district on top of the hill. On the corner, surrounded by green grass and newly planted trees, was the recreation center.

The center was the place where seniors had dinner and attended small concerts, and people flocked to other events of all kinds—flea markets, craft fairs, slide shows. One whole side of the building was a basketball court, and underneath that, on the slope, was a daylight basement. Here the quilters had their headquarters, Aunt Joy had said.

Alice June couldn't see much, looking in—the door was solid wood and the bushes were higher than her head. But she knocked loudly, three times, not sounding timid at all, though her heart was beating unusually fast and her mouth was dry, as though she'd been running. The door opened and there stood Mrs. Lucchetti.

"Well! It's Alice June! Hello, young lady. Hey everybody! Here's our newest member!"

Alice June stood rooted to the sidewalk as numerous heads, most of them white or gray-haired, glanced up from their work at her. A few just looked, but most smiled, or so it seemed. She smiled back and lifted her hand to wave.

"Come on in, child, it's a bit chilly out there," said Mrs. Lucchetti. "Let me introduce you to the club." Alice June stepped in onto the linoleum floor. Fluorescent lights were bright overhead, showing two or three sewing machines against the windows, a long table where some red fabric was laid out, a long kitchen counter with a box of doughnuts on it, a sink, and shelves overhead with boxes and files, cans holding scissors and pencils, and old tins that she later found out held thread and embroidery supplies, measuring tapes, and pins and needles. There were books, too, and magazines, all with pictures of quilts on their covers.

In the middle of the room were four wooden sawhorses, and clamped to them was a large frame made of long, delicate boards, with a thin strip of fabric tacked onto the frame. Pinned to this fabric strip was an enormous quilt top with a layer of white fluffy stuff beneath it and another layer of fabric beneath that. On one side, the quilt was rolled over one of the strips of wood and around this section several ladies were sewing. Mrs. Lucchetti led Alice June to them.

"Alice June, I'd like you to meet Luella," she said, and the lady smiled and nodded, saying "welcome to the club." Alice June thanked her and nodded too, offering her hand in its small black glove. Luella stuck her needle into the quilt, and shook Alice June's hand with her bony one. "Nice to meet you," she said. "We've been hearing about your squares."

One by one, Mrs. Lucchetti introduced her to them all, and Alice June felt she would never remember all their names. There were Joyce, Luella, Lucille, Mimi, Dottie, Betty, Marge, Mrs. Lucchetti of course, Eileen, Elsie, Marion, Effie, and Mrs. Pearl. They all greeted her with a smile and a brief "hello" or "welcome," except for Betty, who just looked up and nodded.

When she came to Mrs. Pearl, Alice June's thoughts went back to the still, sunny day last fall. She recalled the hush in the hall, the echo of the sounds in the valley, and tiny stitches on snow-white cotton. And here was Mrs. Pearl offering Alice June her hand, and speaking to her in a voice that was low and steady.

"We're glad to have you, Alice June. I'd like to see those squares we've been hearing about. Do you have them with you?" Alice June nodded and began to shrug off her backpack. Mrs. Pearl said, "Go ahead and lay them out on top of this one."

Alice June wiggled out of her pack, unzipped the pocket, and carefully pulled out the squares and unwrapped them. Everyone put down their needles and stood up as she laid them out. She couldn't reach very well with the quilt frame up so high on the sawhorses, so Mrs. Lucchetti brought her a stepstool. One by one, the butterfly squares went down on the quilt that was in progress on the frame. The ladies were absolutely quiet. There went the one with the lavender flowers and the one with the green plaid in the wings. There was the one surrounded by daisies, and the one with the bright polka dots with purple stitching around them. Finally, one by one, all 20 were in full view.

It was Betty, the one who hadn't smiled, who spoke in a husky, loud voice, breaking the prolonged silence: "Godalmighty, how old did you tell us the gal was who made these? And when was it?"

Mrs. Lucchetti turned to Alice June, who said, "My great-aunt did them and she died when she was 12. So it was before that. She died before my dad was born, a long time before. My mom told me it was probably about 1930 or so. I don't know exactly."

"Well," said Betty, "these are pretty good. What do you want to do with them?"

"Make a quilt," Alice June said.

"Do you know how?"

"No," said Alice June, "not yet. That's why I'm here."

Betty looked around at the others. "She's a member, is she?"

"We need to get the five dollars from her for the year's dues," replied Mrs. Lucchetti.

"Let's worry about that next time," said Betty, as she rose from her chair and came over to Alice June. Bending forward, she put her hands on the girl's shoulders.

"Little lady, this is a big job," she said in her loud voice. "We'd better get started."

"What do we do first?" Alice June asked.

"Go through those magazines over there and pick out a quilt style you like. Show it to me and I'll figure out about how much fabric you'll need."

Alice looked through a magazine and found a quilt she wanted to use as a model for hers. On it, the appliquéd squares—in other words the decorated ones—were framed by rectangles of a solid color. Narrow strips of fabric separated the framed squares. Where the narrow strips met one another, there was a square of a different color. The narrow strips and squares reached beyond the framed appliqué squares into the border.

"That one?" Betty asked. "It's a little more complicated, but if you're willing to tackle it, so are we."

Alice June was willing.

"Now we make a shopping list. You know what I mean by the main color?" Without waiting for a response, Betty said, "It's the one you'll use the most of. You'll need fabric for the back and the borders, sashing and batting—that's the filling—and so on. Do you want to write it down or shall I?"

"I can," said Alice June.

"Let's get out the measuring tape. What size bed are you trying to cover?"

"A regular double one, I think."

And with that, Betty measured the squares, explaining as she went about seam allowances and sashing, borders and backing, and calling out to Alice June various yardages of main colors and secondary colors and the size and thickness of batting and kinds of thread.

"Let me see the list," Betty said, and inspected it. "Bring this stuff back next week. We'll work on getting the decks cleared." Then, for the first time, she smiled.

List in hand, Alice June climbed out of the car, and, with her mother, opened the door of the fabric store. She was met by the sight of dozens of colorful bolts of cloth, closely packed, stacked in long rows throughout the huge room. She searched the walls and saw painted high in one corner the words "Calico Corner"; this is what Betty had told her to look for. Making a beeline for it, she found muslin and bolt after bolt of small flowery prints and solid colors, grouped by colors and looking, from a distance, like a rainbow.

She checked the list again. "Full-size bed batting." In a bin at the end of a row, she found plastic-wrapped, tightly rolled sheets of light, fluffy white stuffing. Betty had said that in the old days, ladies carded wool or cotton by hand and used that for filling between layers of the quilts. That was why all that close stitching was needed, she said, to keep the batting from shifting around.

Next, Alice June found a spool of quilting thread, an especially strong, tangle-proof thread made of pure cotton. She then located, by poking around and craning her neck, the bolts of solid-colored fabric, which were stacked on shelves that began at about her eye level and rose almost to the ceiling.

"Momma, can you help me get something down? I need white fabric that's 120" wide. Betty said I could use it on the quilt back. I think it's over here." Her mother searched the bolts, tipping them out a little and reading the ends.

"Here it is; look out, it's heavy!"

Momma carefully lifted it down and carried it over to the cutting table while Alice June, with one of Alice Patricia's squares in her hand, went over to the bolts of colored cotton, looking for the perfect shade. She was trying to find three colors: a pale yellow that went with a flowered calico found in quite a few of the old squares, and a lavender that drew out a fabric that there was less of, but which went well with the yellow. And, one more.

Betty had said, "You've got to have an artist's eye, kiddo. Yellow and purple go well together, and so do orange and blue, and red and green. When you get them next to each other, they just look good. Each one makes the other one more intense. They're even called 'complementary colors.'"

She had also told Alice June, "Now, remember, you're the one that has to live with it, so only take my color advice as far as you want to. Looks like you have a good idea already."

The two of them had agreed that those two colors, yellow and lavender, would look nice, and they also reminded Alice June of springtime, which it was now. Outside, a soft spring rain was falling, and trees were starting to "foam," as she called it. When the new leaves were pushing their way out of buds, and blurring the angles of the bare branches with a pale green, it looked like green foam to her. This inspired her choice for the third color: green.

Alice planned to make the framing around the butterfly blocks yellow and the narrow strips of fabric separating the framed squares lavender. Where the lavender strips joined, there would be a square of soft green fabric, called a cornerstone. The strips would be the sashing, which would frame the squares like a wooden sash frames a window.

She loaded the first two bolts into her mother's arms and hitched the third under her own left arm, with the batting held firmly under her right elbow. They made their way to the cutting table, occasionally bumping into one of the closely packed rows of cloth. On the list were the calculations Betty had given her: 3 yards for the back, 5 yards of butter yellow, 1½ yards of lavender, and ¼ yard of the soft green, reminding her of the foamy trees outside. Betty had said, "When you see how it goes together you'll see how we figured it out."

The lady cutting the cloth asked Alice June's mom if she'd been quilting long.

"Not even a second," she replied. "My daughter's decided to learn."

The lady's eyebrows went up. "Really? That's a nice combination of colors. You picked them out, too?"

Alice June nodded and the lady smiled and shook her head. "Well, I guess I won't worry about the future of quilting," she said, "with kids like you coming up. Good luck with it, little gal."

In the car on the way home, Alice June took out the old square again and held it up to the folded fabrics in the big plastic bag on her lap. They were so new, but somehow they fit with the old-fashioned bits and pieces—the knots and swirls of green thread winding through the squares, and the fabrics of the butterflies. She had been told by Betty to wash the new fabrics by machine, with hot water and soap, and dry them in the dryer on high to shrink them down and soften them up. "Get that damn sizing out," is what Betty had said, and "shrink 'em before you get 'em sewed in, not after." That made sense to Alice June.

A thought suddenly came to her. "Momma," she began, "How will I get all this stuff to the center from school on Monday? And how will I carry it all day long?"

"Mmmmm." Her mom was thinking. But before she could speak, Alice June questioned, "Do you think we could leave it at Aunt Joy's? Then maybe Mrs. Lucchetti could bring it over, if I asked her with a pleeeaaase."

"I think so. Let's check. In fact, let's drop in and say hi and ask in person, while we're out and about."

Momma swung the car around on the quiet road that ran by the pasture near the fairgrounds. "You always seem to think of a way," she said and smiled, her eyes on the road.

Alice June, tightly clutching the old square, held it up to the window, open just a little at the top, and then pressed it to her face. The cool spring air was still in it and it smelled like the wind at this time of year, fresh, clean, a little damp with the quiet rain that was still gently falling. It was just the kind of day, with its bright, diffused light and soft, steady drizzle, that would be perfect for quilting.

CHAPTER NINE

As AGREED, Mrs. Lucchetti brought the fabric and the rest of the quilt makings to Monday's meeting. When Alice June arrived from the bus, Betty was already examining the material as though she were a detective looking for clues.

"Did it shrink much?" she was asking Mrs. Lucchetti. "Or bleed color?"

"Not so's you'd notice," Mrs. Lucchetti replied. "Don't you think it has a nice feel? Easy to needle. Hey, here's the youngest member herself. Do you want to cut it up yourself or let me do it?"

"Cut it up?" Alice June's eyes opened wide with some alarm.

"I don't mean into ribbons," Mrs. Lucchetti laughed, "Just into the sizes we need. Let's measure up and get going."

Alice June took the quilting magazine off the shelf where she had left it and opened it to the pattern she had chosen. The three bent their heads over it.

"Are you good at math?" asked Betty.

"I think so," said Alice June, "but which kind? Algebra? Geometry? Arithmetic?"

"Plain old arithmetic. You need to add half an inch all around whatever you are cutting, because there is going to be a one-quarter-inch seam allowance along every edge of every one of your pieces."

She laid out a square from the scrap table and folded under about a quarter of an inch on all sides. "See? You have to allow for the stitching."

Alice June stepped back a moment. It was becoming clear, she was thinking, that a quilter had to be not just handy with a needle, but something more . . . something almost like. . . .

"Engineers, honey, that's what we've got to be. Quilts are engineered like bridges or something. You get off by a quarter inch and multiply that along seven feet of squares and pretty soon it's all caty-wampus. You have to be very precise. Nowadays we have these graph-style cutting mats. Let me show you."

Mrs. Lucchetti peeled a piece of fabric off from a table, and underneath it was a large mat of what looked like hard green rubber. It was printed with yellow ruled lines intersecting all over it. Mrs. Lucchetti picked up a tool with a round blade. It looked like a pizza cutter.

"Now this is perfect for those rectangles and squares you want to do," she said. "Lay the fabric down along these lines, and then put a ruler along the side, measuring in at the width you want. Run the blade along the edge of the ruler, and poof! You've got a strip, just like that."

"What did they do in the old days?" Alice June asked.

"Well, they just did their best. A lot of quilts got measured out with yardsticks or measuring tapes or maybe pieces of yarn or twigs or who knows what all, out in the yard on the lawn in the good weather and cut on kitchen tables or the floor, if you had one. Those old gals with sod huts and dirt floors—with snakes falling down from the ceiling—I don't know for sure what they did. But they managed, somehow, and came up with some beautiful quilts. It's amazing, what came out of that time, absolutely amazing what you can do if you have to. Anyway, we need to figure out the measurements for all of your pieces."

She took a piece of paper and, with Alice June looking over her shoulder, calculated the needed length and width of the yellow rectangles, explaining as she went.

"OK, now you figure out the rest."

"You mean the lavender sashing?"

"Yes, that's a start, and also the cornerstones and binding. You'll need the border, too. That needs to be cut 2½" wide. But I'll show you when you get to it."

So it went, Mrs. Lucchetti explaining and showing until Alice June had the idea. Alice June sat down with paper and pencil and drew a picture of the quilt top, and after a few starts and stops and some erasing, brought her calculations back to Mrs. Lucchetti, who nodded. "Looks right to me."

Betty showed her how to lay the fabric on the cutting mat, straighten the ends, and measure and cut first her strips and then the rectangles. Alice June carefully cut, counted, and stacked the different colors and shapes of fabric, folded the border fabric, and, suddenly feeling very tired, walked over to Mrs. Lucchetti and Betty. They were bent over another quilt, a red-white-and-blue Texas Star, which was already in a frame.

"What else do I need to do?" she asked.

"Sit down and have a graham cracker," Mrs. Lucchetti said, "and some juice. You've done enough for one day. Next week, you'll start sewing it all together. Do you have a sewing machine?"

"I think Momma has one in the closet," Alice June offered.

"Well, you can use one of ours. What I want to know is, can you run one?"

"I can learn," Alice June said and folded her arms, her feet wide apart, in a stance that was a mixture of fatigue and determination.

Both ladies laughed. "You'll do. See you next week."

AT HOME, there was a letter on the table in the hall. Alice June recognized Uncle Bobbie's handwriting. His letters, before these last few months, had been rare and always addressed to her parents. This one, like the notes with the keepsakes, was addressed just to her. She opened it carefully and read:

Dear Alice June,

I hope you and your folks are well. I think of you all often. I wanted to tell you I went up to the old homestead this morning. Funny to think of an old man like me breaking the law, but I took my old self over a fence that had a "No Trespassing" sign on it. After all, the only living things up there now are a bunch of cows and they didn't seem to mind me much. I don't know what got into me; I haven't been up there for years. But I remembered, I guess, how pretty it is up there in the springtime.

The trees are beginning to bloom in town, and I thought about the apple trees our father planted and wondered how big they were getting, if they were still standing at all. My trip up the lane was muddy and I had to stop a bit to rest, but I think the effort was well rewarded. It was a very pretty sight that met my eyes as I rounded the corner and saw the little orchard. The two trees that stand in front of where the house used to be were especially beautiful, full of blossoms, and they smelled as sweet as they used to. Isn't it funny how smells bring back memories?

The only sound was the creek; it has some water in it now that it is spring, and the wind of course. It seems it has always blown through that little valley with just the same sound. I thought of Alice Patricia and how she used to sit under those trees with Stubby and do her sewing. Because you are interested in her I wanted to tell you about it.

There is not much news, really. Mr. Gould, down the street, lost his hound to old age and he always said he would never get another dog. But I see a puppy in his yard now. I wonder how he will keep up with it. He was a grown-up, so it seemed, when I was a boy, which would make him nearly a hundred, well, maybe not quite that old, but almost. Maybe this dog will keep him young.

The school yard is starting to liven up now that spring is here. They had baseball practice yesterday and today. Well, all for now. I hope your weather is as nice as ours is.

Love,

Uncle Bobbie

ALICE JUNE'S MOTHER stood by the stove as Alice June read the letter, and looked over at her as she folded it up and slowly replaced it in the envelope.

"How is Uncle Bobbie?" Momma asked.

"I think he's fine. He must be; he climbed over a fence and trespassed to see the old homestead again. How old did you say he is?"

"I think he's just a little under 80 or so," said Momma. "But he's fairly spry."

Alice June thought for a moment. Then, "Momma, who owns the quilt I'm working on?"

"I've been meaning to talk to Aunt Joy and your dad about that. But I think I know what they'll say."

"What will they say?"

"Well, I'll bet they'll want to give it to you for your hope chest. After all, you'll have a home of your own someday and maybe children you could pass it on to. And you're the one who's really taken an interest in it. But of course, I'll need to check and make sure."

Alice June was quiet. She held the letter with one hand, and with the other rubbed a hole in the steam on the kitchen window. Her eyes were open wide, and they stung with tears. She looked out on the damp, cool gray sky of early twilight, her eyes falling on the apple tree, with its buds growing fatter by the day. Rain sparkled on the branches, and the lacy silhouettes of the more distant trees were black against the western clouds.

Her tears began to splash on the sill, and she felt her mother's arm around her waist.

"I'll talk to them soon," she said, and for a moment tightened her hand on Alice June, who nodded without a word and pressed her hot cheek against the cold glass. Then Momma walked away quietly, the sounds of her footsteps growing fainter down the hall.

Alice June stood with her face to the window, and whispered so quietly, only she could hear. Or perhaps someone else, somewhere, would hear too.

"Someday, I'll go up to the homestead with you. Please wait for me, and stay spry."

TRUE TO HER WORD, Alice June did learn to use a sewing machine, though she had never seen one outside of her mother's closet. It took a lot of time just to memorize threading, winding the bobbin, and adjusting the tension. And there was still a lot to learn. The machine had to be cleaned, oiled, and dusted now and then, and occasionally the thread would catch, jam, and break, and there were other aggravations, mostly having to do with the bobbin. More than once, her patience grew so thin she felt like throwing the fabric down and stamping her feet. But Betty really wanted her to learn the machine the right way the first time, and Alice June knew it was important not just for this project but for future ones. So she stuck with it. She was using an older machine, from the 1950s. Betty said, "All you need for this is forward and reverse, none of the fancy stuff. There's less to go wrong with these old workhorse machines and they're built to last."

The newer machines were plastic and had lots of fancy embroidery stitches and a million different features, but Alice June was glad to be using the simpler model. She liked the way it looked, too, in its cherrywood cabinet that it folded down into. Both the cabinet and the machine, which was black decorated all over with gold scrolling, were slim, graceful, and elegant.

When she sat down and began sewing the yellow frames around the butterfly blocks, she found she felt fairly comfortable with the machine. She began to relax a little and enjoy the humming of the little motor, and she liked watching the fabric pass under the silver foot. She had to work at keeping the seams even, but she was getting the hang of it and even got a nod of approval from Betty and Mrs. Lucchetti on the straightness of her seams.

AFTER A MONTH of weekly club meetings, steadily stitching and pressing, as early spring unfolded into warmer days and later dusks, the quilt top was ready to have the quilting pattern marked onto it and be put together with the batting and the back. It had to be pinned to the mattress ticking on the frame, and the frame placed, each corner on the back of a sawhorse, in the center of the room. Then came the basting, long stitches done by hand to keep the three layers together without slipping or shifting as the quilting began. Alice June was pleased to find her youth was a real plus now, as it was good to have someone on the floor, under the quilt, to pull the basting needles through to the bottom and push them up again in the center, where the ladies would pick them up and push them down again in another spot. This was in the center of the quilt, where the ladies could not reach to do it all themselves. She was new enough at it that she had to concentrate, but somehow it was relaxing too, the careful easing in any extra fullness, the even distribution of the top, holding it carefully as the long basting stitches went through all the layers and back up again. It was rhythmic and soothing after a while. She would think, "The little rabbit goes down, the little rabbit comes up," as the needle disappeared and reappeared, carrying the thread behind it.

Always, each time she saw the squares, she was reminded of Alice Patricia, and she wondered if her great-aunt would have liked the colors and the way they brought out the prints in the butterflies. Alice June especially loved the little squares of green and how they looked like jewels dropped onto the fabric. Like any pretty picture, the butterflies looked even prettier in their "frames."

SHE OFTEN THOUGHT, too, of Uncle Bobbie and his visit to the homestead. She hadn't heard from him since, though she'd written him a note. At times she thought she could almost feel the warm sweet wind of that part of the country, scented with pine and fresh earth, and imagine, in the old days, quilts and linens hanging on the clothesline at the homestead, drying fast in the breezes, with Alice Patricia and Stubby nearby, and Uncle Bobbie playing, maybe at the creek or in the barn. Strange how she had never been there, only heard about it, yet it seemed she could almost remember it. Maybe it was just imagining, but how could it seem so real? This particular day, her daydream was interrupted and her mind brought back to the present by Betty.

"Well, young lady," she said, her hands clasped before her, "stand back and look at that."

Finally, the layers were basted together and the actual quilting was ready to begin. Seventy-three inches across, eighty-nine inches long, the squares and the sashing stretched on the frame in front of her. Next, it would be rolled onto one side of the frame and only two feet or so exposed at a time, along the long side, so that the quilters could get at their work.

Alice June took a long look and with a satisfied smile, turned to Betty. "I like it."

"Me too," Betty said, grinning, "She's a beaut."

Mrs. Lucchetti had walked up to join them, her arms crossed, and smiled. She nodded approval at Alice June. "Nice work."

"Let's get started on the quilting now, OK?" Alice June asked.

"I guess we could, if you're that anxious," Betty said with a laugh. "Ladies, thread your needles."

ONE OF THE THINGS Betty and Mrs. Lucchetti had insisted on was that Alice June learn to use a thimble. "Better now than later," they both said. So she had gradually gotten used to the feeling while basting and found that it did make it easier. Otherwise, the tiny needle would puncture her skin, and even her fingernails, if she tried to push several stitches through the layers. She was discovering that sewing involved a degree of pain, with the inevitable needle sticks, and sometimes a drop of blood, which could stain the fabric. So, adhesive bandages were a part of any well-equipped sewing kit.

Alice June unscrewed the C-clamps from the corners of the frame and, with Betty on the other end, they rolled the quilt carefully over the long strip of wood until a two-foot width remained. Then Alice June tightened the clamps again and scooted the sawhorses closer together. They threaded their needles, sat down, and began, with a goal of six to eight stitches per inch, to quilt along the pattern lines Alice June had traced in sewing pencil (which would wash out easily later).

This was, she felt, really the beginning of it, what she had been waiting for, and her heart quickened as she sat down to actually quilt for the first time. After this part, which was the most time-consuming stage of the process, the binding would be sewn on, and the quilt would be completed.

They sat, Betty, Mrs. Lucchetti, and Alice June, and quilted in the slanting golden sun, saying very little. Finally the sun was gone, and only the pink of the sky behind the old church across the street remained.

"Better give it up for tonight, little gal," said Betty. "We've got a good start. We'll have to turn on all the overheads if we stay any longer, and we might as well quit. Daylight's easier for my eyes, that's for sure."

Mrs. Lucchetti spoke up, "Next week some of the others will be done with that project they've got going in the other room, and they'll lend a hand, I'll bet you."

"How will I pay them back?" asked Alice June.

"You'll help them on their projects. That's how the club works. It makes it easier and more fun for everybody," Betty said.

"They won't care that my stitches aren't perfect?"

Mrs. Lucchetti and Betty both laughed, and Betty spoke up. "Perfection may be a goal, but less than perfect will do. Besides," she added, "You're doing very well."

Alice June knew by now that Betty gave compliments sparingly, and she blushed with pleasure at the praise. All she could think of to say was, delivered with a smile, "Well, I guess I'll see you next week, then."

"Sure enough. We'll be here, with bells on. Good night, little lady."

CHAPTER TEN

WHAT DO YOU DO at the quilters' club?" Lindsay asked one Friday night, as they were both getting sleepy in Lindsay's bed under the eaves. Lulu, Lindsay's Boston terrier, lay between them, softly snoring.

"Well, it depends on what day. We're working on the actual quilting now. That's when you stitch the top, bottom, and middle together by hand with teeny-tiny stitches. Some people use a sewing machine to quilt but I wanted to do it by hand."

"How come?"

"I just think it's prettier. And it's harder. I really want to get good and do it the old-fashioned way."

"You like lots of old-fashioned things," Lindsay said. "How come?"

Alice June thought about that for a minute, her hands pillowing her head. "I'm not sure," she said, "I just do."

"Well, I think it's cool," Lindsay said. "I don't have anything old-fashioned. I don't even know where my family came from a long time ago. Nobody remembers, I guess. I don't know anybody else whose great-great-grandma came out on the Oregon Trail."

"I didn't know I knew anybody like that either, 'til Mom told me just last fall," replied Alice June. "Probably lots of people have relatives who did and they just don't know."

"I've been thinking," said Lindsay. "If I wanted to learn to quilt, would you teach me?"

"Sure," said Alice June, without hesitating.

"I thought maybe a pillow to start with," Lindsay said. "For my mom, for Mother's Day, or sometime."

"That would be a good way to start," said Alice June, drifting off a little more.

"Can we take the bus to the fabric store tomorrow?"

"Sure, or maybe Momma would take us," said Alice June. "I just have to get my work done first."

"I'll help you," offered Lindsay.

"It's a deal," said Alice June, very sleepily.

"Maybe if she likes it I could make one for Aunt Sandy," Lindsay said, sounding very awake.

"Prob'ly . . . you could. . . ."

"And if she likes that, I could make one for my grandma," said Lindsay, "Maybe you could show me how to embroider an iguana on it."

Alice June was quiet except for regular breathing.

"Well," Lindsay said, mostly to herself, "if you didn't laugh at that one, you must really be asleep. I'll have to talk to myself instead. Good night, Alice June."

AFTER THE LETTER about the homestead Uncle Bobbie had sent, the packages stopped for several weeks, though Alice June still got an occasional little note from him, just a newsy hello. Then, in early May, another package arrived. It was larger and heavier than any of the other things, arriving in a sturdy cardboard box stamped "Insured" in red letters. Inside, padded with tissue and wrapped in brown paper, was a wooden box about a foot square, with a lid needlepointed in gently faded flowers. The dark brown wood was fine-grained and old, like the tick-tock clock on the mantelpiece, and when she lifted the lid with its stitched roses, leaves, and pansies, she drew in her breath sharply. It was a sewing box.

Opening it carefully, with wonder, she lifted the delicately hinged lid. A shallow wooden shelf with a number of small compartments filled the top of the box and held old wooden spools of cotton and silk thread, cards of pins and of needles, a small silver thimble, tiny gleaming gold-handled scissors, and a measuring tape, frayed and worn. This shelf lifted out and, gently, she set it down on the kitchen table beside the box. Underneath it, on the worn green velvet lining, were scraps of fabric, a few of which she recognized, a small red tin of mismatched buttons, and a tangled pile of gaily colored embroidery thread.

There was a small round pincushion of blue calico, obviously homemade, on the floor of the box, and attached to it by a short black cord was a tiny little cone-shaped bag, of the same fabric, closed at the top and very hard. It felt like it had sand in it. She had never seen a pincushion that looked quite like this one. It was soft, except for the little cone, and had something that looked like wool fleece sticking out at the top where the stitches drew the fabric together. A few pins were still in it. And that was everything, except for an envelope with her name on it.

Dear Alice June,

This was the last thing I found in the attic that had belonged to Alice Patricia. Our father made this box for her, and our mother needlepointed the top. The wood came from a black walnut tree that grew on Dad's father's farm. So I guess it is probably about as much of a family keepsake as a person could find. I remember very well her sitting and sewing with this box open beside her.

You know, Alice June, you and I don't know each other all that well, because I haven't seen you very often. But the fact that you are interested in your great-aunt tells me a lot about you. I have thought about her so much all these years, but even more since you asked me about her, and the memories that have come back across time are both bitter and sweet.

These memories are sweet because she was so kind and we loved each other as much as little kids can do, and the memories are bitter too because she died so young, and so much of her short life was affected by her weak heart. When she was barely 12, she begged to be allowed out of bed to dance around the Maypole, you know, the old-fashioned kind of May Day celebration. May is always so pretty here, my favorite month, and when we were small it was even more beautiful, with songbirds such as bluebirds and meadowlarks so plentiful, not like now, when there are so few. They would sing from every fencepost then, so it seemed. Pine Creek, the one that runs through town in that curving gully that is usually dry, would rush down from the mountain as the snow melted, a beautiful clear green that danced and sparkled in the sun. Everywhere lilacs and roses were blooming, and the whole town smelled like them. I don't think my picture of it is only the nostalgic memory of a child. It was truly beautiful.

That first day of May was so lovely, and she begged so hard to dance even a little, that our mother and father finally gave in. She danced two or three times around the circle and felt weak, and went home to bed. She never got up again, and died a few days later. I was eight years old then, and I remember it like it was yesterday.

In our few years together I got to know her as well as any little brother could. She didn't go to school after the sickness that damaged her heart, and so was home for me to tag along with, and pester some too, probably. I might have played a few mischievous tricks on her, as little brothers will do, not meaning any harm, but I did some things I am ashamed of now. Once I pushed her off the fence, and she struggled to get her air back, and she turned a little blue. I didn't know it would hurt her. I got in big trouble, but I already felt very sorry. Maybe I was jealous because she never had to work hard at the chores, and she got some attention I didn't. I was too young to understand why things were the way they were.

She was a young girl like any other, with all the thoughts and hopes and dreams you would expect. She felt frustrated, I am sure, and once in a while she would cry about all the things she used to do and now could not. But mostly, she was so brave. And, she put so much of her love and her imagination into her sewing. You could see from her butterflies, which I remember well, how playful she was at heart.

She would sing songs to me after she blew out the candle at night, in the bedroom we shared. Her voice was very pretty. She wanted to grow up and get married, like the other girls, and make lots of quilts, so she told me. Nowadays, maybe they could have fixed her heart and let her live, maybe to be older even than me. But back then, lots of people died very young.

I've always been sentimental. When I was in the army during the war, and later, during the long hours I spent working for the railroad, I spent lots of time thinking about the old homestead and our little family. And I still do.

Because we live far apart, it's hard to visit often enough to really stay in touch. That is one reason I am so glad you asked me about your great-aunt. That started us writing to one another. You are family, too, and I feel lucky to be getting to know you better and to be your great-uncle. So, thank you for asking about Alice Patricia and bringing back my memories again. I want you to have this box, because I feel sure that you will love, use, and appreciate it more than anyone else I know.

Love,

Uncle Bobbie

As the weeks slipped by and spring began to drift toward summer, the quilters' club drew close to finishing Alice June's quilt. Alice June had brought the sewing box to show them, and to ask them about the funny cone-shaped thing. Mrs. Lucchetti, after she and all the rest had admired the box and laughingly warned, "You'd better keep a close eye on it," had said the little bag attached to the pincushion was a "strawberry," containing emery or sand, to poke needles into to sharpen them. So Alice June had decided to take the pincushion to the club in her pack every Monday and use it to keep her needles sharp, and she found it helped.

The quilters had taken much time and care, not simply sewing diagonal lines across the quilt blocks or following traced lines, but taking at least six to eight stitches to the inch, they had quilted all around the butterflies and squares and then went on to take liberties, as creative people are likely to do. They began to invent their own designs and, freehand, stitched dragonflies, flowers, leaves, and more butterflies in the plain squares; and on the borders, leaves, vines, daisies, snails, and even more butterflies.

Mrs. Lucchetti outlined a frog; Betty, a garter snake; and all of it was in careful white stitching, so you had to look closely to see what it was. For some reason, this was a playful quilt, so they said, and they felt freer than usual to go "out of bounds"—that is, working without a pattern and being inventive. There was a lot of smiling and quiet laughter around the quilt on those Monday afternoons. Soft spring rains might be knocking the frail blossoms off the cherry trees outside the basement windows, or a stiff breeze off the water might be blowing them around, or a pale sun, growing stronger every day, might be shining on the wet earth, warming it and drawing the flowers up and out to drink in the light; but whatever the weather, it seemed sunny in the daylight basement. It was almost as though a gentle enchantment lay lightly over this quilt.

Even Effie and Lucille, who had never had much to say to each other (Mrs. Lucchetti said they had had a grudge since high school, "probably over a boy named George," she added), were seen chatting amiably at the edge of the quilt one day.

Alice June, struggling to learn fine sewing, would lift her tired head on its stiff neck and look in turn at each of the ladies, wondering sometimes about their long histories and lives. What had the world been like when they were her age? Sometimes they would talk about it and she loved those times;

she would sit and sew quietly and take it in like a sponge, just listening. Often the conversation would begin with, "Do you remember?"

"Do you remember," Mimi said to Luella one day, "when the war was on and we all pooled gas coupons and went to Seattle? And missed the last ferry home and slept all night in the waiting room? Boy, was Seattle ever hopping then."

"Oh, yes, and the boys. So many handsome boys in uniform, you couldn't imagine it."

"Do you remember the USO jeep coming our houses, to take all the single young women to the dances? And how the boys outnumbered us ten to one?"

There would be a laugh and then someone would say "Those were the days," and then they would be quiet for a little while.

THERE WAS A LOT OF TRADING GOING ON, memories, recipes, household hints, gardening news, now and then an update on a favorite TV show, and some complaining, too, about the government, the weather, unreliable repairmen, rheumatism, glasses that didn't fit, and hearing that "wasn't what it used to be." There would be a little polite bragging about the grades and accomplishments of grandchildren and occasionally a gripe about "these young people don't know their manners anymore," which worried Alice June a little, but she figured they must not mean her. And, unfailingly, they quilted for her and with her on the quilt made from Alice Patricia's squares.

Though she didn't have words for it then, she felt they were on her side, and she gradually, almost without knowing it, became a part of this ladies' circle, seeing their differences and their likenesses, their kindness, their skills, and the hints of sadness she sometimes saw in them as they talked about times and people that were gone. She would visualize them as young girls like her, only in different, old-fashioned dresses and high-topped shoes like in the old books, in this old town when horses still sometimes drew wagons down the streets.

Of course not all the ladies were old enough to have been around way back then; some were younger, her mom's age even, and they talked about their "old times" too. But the older ones interested her more, almost like they were a bridge to another world. And so they were. From them, she was learning skills taught to them by mothers and grandmothers whose fathers and husbands had gone off to the Civil War, so she heard them saying one day.

But mostly, they looked ahead and around, not dwelling solely on the past. They talked of politics and yoga and computers too, among other things. These long spring afternoons brought her not just the completion of the quilt, but a circle of friends who, despite their age difference of many years, had something important in common with her.

They all loved creating something beautiful and useful with their hands, something that would be treasured for a long, long time.

FINALLY THE DAY CAME when the last quilting stitches went in. At that meeting, Alice June held her breath a lot, as it wasn't clear they would finish. She could see it would be a close race. But as the afternoon turned the corner toward evening, she ran out of room to stitch in her little section, and so did Elsie, who quilted smack dab up to Alice June's stitches, and the same thing was happening all over this last strip of quilt. Finally, Betty laid down her needle and announced, "That's it, kid," and Mrs. Lucchetti said, "You did it," and Alice June, with a grin wide enough to chase all the tired hours away, replied, "No, *we* did it."

"Hey, everybody," Betty raised her voice to say, "Alice's quilt is quilted." A cheer went up in the room, from those around Effie's quilt as well as those ladies around Alice's own, and from the women standing at the stove and the sink chatting, and from one pouring her coffee and two working at the sewing machines. As they laid down their needles and whatever they were doing, a quiet round of applause began and circled the room until it filled the air, and kept going. Through it all Alice June smiled, blushed, and looked down at Alice Patricia's handiwork, the butterfly wings surrounded by hundreds of careful stitches put in place with so much care and love, and whispered so low that no one could hear, "I wish you were here, too." She waited a moment, and said one more very quiet thing. "In a way, you are."

On to the business at hand, as usual, Betty was already removing the C-clamps at the corners of the long thin pieces of trim wood that held the quilt, and rolling the frame back to unpin the quilt at the edges. Suddenly Mrs. Lucchetti stopped and raised her hand.

"Hey, everybody," she said, speaking loudly. "Let's wait a minute before we fold it up, and take a good look at it in all its glory. After all, this is a special occasion."

And so they did. Stretched out its full length and width, with still enough pins to hold it to the frame, it caught the light and shadows of the low sun in its many curving rows of close, careful stitching, and the butterflies seemed to lift themselves out from the background as though they wanted to fly. Everyone in the room gathered to admire it, crowding about and gently touching the fabric, lightly tracing the butterfly feelers and remarking on the beauty of this quilt.

Alice June just stood and smiled, nodding her thanks. The culmination of all the weeks and months of exhausting handwork, sometimes grinding and tedious, so many hours of careful labor, now lay completed. And she knew that the love that went into these stitches would stay.

Standing there, looking down at the quilt and then up at her fellow quilters, she silently thanked them from the bottom of her heart. She felt too shy to say more than a simple "thank you," out loud, now. But she resolved to stay on with the quilters' club, not just because she wanted to, not just because she would make more quilts of her own, but to help them as they had helped her.

She knew she would work with these ladies for years to come, learning not just their many skills, but also the lessons of loyalty, teamwork, and the love that friends have for one another when they work together to create something beautiful and lasting.

Now it was time to fold up the quilt, after all the pins were out and the quilt was free of the frame. Effie, Betty, Mrs. Lucchetti, and Alice June each held one of the corners and brought them together, folding the quilt in half lengthwise. With just Alice June and Betty left, they folded it lengthwise again and then, a corner in each hand, met in the middle and folded it twice more. At the next meeting, she would begin the task of sewing on the binding, a folded strip of material to be sewn by machine to the top and then turned under and sewn by hand, with nearly invisible stitches, on the back. It would probably take at least two meetings to complete it.

Sure enough, three weeks went by, and two meeting times of hand sewing. Once again she had help, but most of the binding stitches were her own. Then the quilt was carefully folded again, and as Alice June held open a large shopping bag, Mrs. Lucchetti and Betty packed the quilt into it for her. She held it to her chest with both arms, and it covered her face, too, until all that could be seen were her eyes. She asked, just to be sure, "I do come back again, right?"

Betty answered quickly, "Of course, little gal. You don't get off that easy. We're expecting you to join the troops on Effie's quilt. She has a deadline, you know."

"OK," Alice June replied, relieved. "I shall return." Her serious voice was muffled by the huge shopping bag, and both the ladies laughed.

"You do that," they said. "Now scoot and get that pretty thing home."

And pretty it was. The delicate stitches made tiny shadows and highlights, and Alice Patricia's butterflies seemed to dance over the fabric's surface as if on a breeze. It was beautiful.

Alice June's mother thought so too, when she saw it spread out on the bed. She looked at it for at least a full minute without speaking, her arms crossed, and finally turned her head to Alice June, with a smile, and said,

"I knew you'd find a way. And you did. It's lovely. What will you do with it now?"

"Is it really mine?"

"Yes, Aunt Joy and your dad both said so," Mom replied. "Didn't I tell you that?"

"Yes, but I just wanted to make sure." She hesitated a second. "Can I do anything I want with it?"

Momma looked a little puzzled. "Well, I suppose so. Anything that won't hurt it, anyway. What do you have in mind?"

"Oh, nothing. I was just wondering." But in her mind she was thinking of a place over the mountains, and of a return home.

CHAPTER ELEVEN

*S*CHOOL LET OUT on a June day that began heavy with dew, the grass high and still too wet to mow, deep, shaggy, and emerald green, spread out like thick frosting in all directions under the apple tree by the back door.

The tree was completely leafed out and tiny fruit was forming. When Alice June left for school that morning, she passed close by the tree and thought, as she saw it, of the trees up on the old homestead. Was their fruit bigger? Smaller? She knew that spring came earlier there. They'd been studying latitudes at school, and on the map she could see it was quite a bit farther south. Already it would be hot there and crickets would be singing at night.

She had heard from Uncle Bobbie only once since the letter that accompanied the sewing box. Where that letter was long, the latest one was short, and newsy, a note about the weather and the neighbor's new dog, bigger now and digging under the fence, keeping his master on the ready, as Uncle Bobbie had predicted. School would soon be out. Recently his close friend had died; he just slipped that in. He wrote simply, "I miss him every day."

She had answered the earlier letter but not the latest one, not yet. As she boarded the bus and friends called out to her, she promised herself she would write to Uncle Bobbie as soon as she got home. After, that is, the quilters' meeting. They had decided to meet again on Thursday because Effie was trying to get her quilt done for a graduation gift.

At the meeting Mrs. Lucchetti asked her, "How's that pretty quilt holding up?"

"Really good," said Alice June. "It should—it's still in my mom's cedar chest."

"Why don't you use it?"

"Well," Alice June replied, "I'm worried something might happen to it."

"Ah," Mrs. Lucchetti said, "I see. Such as?"

"I might tear it with my jeans," Alice June replied, "or spill hot chocolate on it."

At that, Mrs. Lucchetti rolled her eyes, and said, "My husband drank coffee in bed every morning, and wine in bed every night, and he snored so loud I thought the roof of the house would blow off." Mrs. Lucchetti laughed then, and the two ladies standing near her laughed, too. But Alice June knew—Aunt Joy had told her—that Mrs. Lucchetti really missed her husband. He had been short, Italian, and smiled a lot, a wood-carver who had mowed the lawn around her treasured flowerbeds, and had died doing just that, on a summer day years ago.

"Well," Mrs. Lucchetti said, "you'll get around to it someday, I reckon. And you'll discover there's nothing like a handmade quilt to give you good dreams."

After the meeting, Alice June watched the rain, driven by a light wind, begin to hit the car windows as Momma took her home. She was thinking about what to write to Uncle Bobbie and realized she needed to talk to her parents first, to ask them something. That evening they would both be home for dinner and she decided that, though she was nervous about it, she had to ask them today. It was too easy to just let the days go by without asking because she had no idea what they would say, and she was afraid the answer would be no. She didn't want to hear that and so kept putting it off. But what if she waited too long?

"Dad," she began, butterflies in her stomach, as they sat down together, "are we taking any vacations this summer?"

"Well, we've been talking about that trip to Montana to see your mom's old friend," he said.

Momma spoke up. "And there's marine science camp for you in July."

"Other than that, we haven't discussed it, really," said her father. "June just came so quickly."

To Alice June, the month of June seemed to have taken forever to arrive, as she sat in school during the warm spring days listening to lawnmowers outside and being too often bored silly in class.

Now was the time and she heard herself say, her heart pounding in her ears, "Could we take a trip to see Uncle Bobbie?"

Her parents looked at each other with some surprise. Mom put her fork down and said, "We hadn't thought of going this year, but I don't really see why not," and, looking across the table at Alice June's dad, "What do you think?"

"I'd have to ask for time off at work, but I always like to go there," he replied, "and Uncle Bobbie isn't getting any younger. I don't imagine they'd object to giving me a couple of days off." Then, looking at Alice June intently, he said, "You've never asked to go there before and I wasn't sure you liked it. You're always so quiet when we're there and there aren't any other kids around. Is there some particular reason you want to go?"

"Yes," she said, and looked down at her hands, clenched in her lap. "I want to take him the quilt."

"To show him?" Momma asked. Her dad was leaning forward, his dinner getting cold, his head cocked, listening.

"No," Alice June replied. "To give him."

66

Her parents were silent for what seemed like forever, watching her without blinking. The clock ticked and bonged and the rain drummed lightly on the window.

"Are you sure you want to?" Mom asked, finally, very quietly. "You worked so hard on it. It's so beautiful."

"You said it was mine to do what I wanted with," she answered. "And this is what I want. She was . . . she was his sister. He remembers her sewing outside with her dog. He remembers her singing to him when he was little, and he remembers the day she died. He sent me her picture and her scrapbook and her sewing box. He sent me almost everything he had left of her. He wrote me that he still misses her. He should have the quilt." She lifted her chin, her eyes glistening with tears. "Are you going to let me?"

Her mom looked again at her dad. "It's your family heirloom," she said, "you decide."

He said only, "Alice June, I'm very, very proud of you. When shall we go?"

THE RANKS OF the quilters' club thinned a little in the summertime, but not a great deal. People had visiting grandkids and family vacations, or just wanted to be outdoors in their gardens. Even so, there was a lot of work going on, as several quilts were under way for the quilt show coming up in September, the same one Alice June had gone to the year before for the first time. Back then, she had looked at the ladies and their creations from a distance; now, she knew them both better.

She knew the quilting itself literally from the inside out—the different kinds of batting and how to tie "invisible" knots that would pull through the fabric and anchor in the batting. She knew the basting process and the pinning and the removal of the quilt from the frame for quilting in the big hoops many of the ladies had at home, or the rolling of the quilt around the big frame for several ladies to work on at once, as they had done for hers.

She had learned, too, about several of her fellow quilters, especially the ones that had become her friends.

There was Mrs. Lucchetti, of course, who had taken her under her wing at the start. And Betty, who was less like a mother hen and more like a porcupine, thought Alice June: a few barbs if you rubbed her the wrong way, but soft on the inside, that was easy to tell.

Listening carefully through the many quiet conversations around her own quilt and those of the others, she had heard a great deal.

One rainy April afternoon, Effie had asked Mrs. Lucchetti about growing artichokes. Everyone knew her husband had had a big vegetable garden, a real Italian kitchen garden with herbs and fig trees, too. Mrs. Lucchetti often answered questions about it and about her own special hobby, which was growing roses. But for some reason, that day, she kept on talking.

"You know, Gene brought the starts for those fig trees home from the war in his duffel bag. He got them from a tree in the village his father and mother had come from. He was born here, you know, but his parents were both from the same little town in Italy. He never knew just how they felt about him fighting the Italians for America, but in general they were proud of him, he knew that.

"I'll never forget how we met, just after he was home from the war. It was on the New York subway. I was 27 and figured I was an old maid, living at home with my parents still, and teaching school in Queens. He was still in uniform and said he was going to go to college on the GI bill. It wasn't love at first sight, but almost.

"He came out West with the Army Corps of Engineers to build dams on the Columbia, and one Sunday drove to the coast to stick his toe in the Pacific. Then he called me from a pay phone and said to pack up the kids and the house, because we were moving west. That is, if I didn't mind. I didn't mind."

All of this poured out of her, with the room so quiet you could hear the pins drop and the gentle rain falling. Then she said, "I guess I'm getting old and sentimental," and was silent again.

ALICE JUNE FELT she already knew Mrs. Lucchetti a little better than she did the others, because she had been to her house. Once, while she and Momma were stopping by at Aunt Joy's, Mrs. Lucchetti had phoned to say she was just taking a pie out of the oven and needed help eating it.

"Alice June and her mom are here, too," Aunt Joy said into the telephone, and held the phone away from her ear with a grin as Mrs. Lucchetti's raised voice boomed its reply, "All the better. Bring them on over. If they like pie, that is."

"Do you like pie?" Aunt Joy asked. Alice June and her mom just looked at one another and grinned.

MRS. LUCCHETTI'S HOUSE was warm, and flowered wallpaper hung in every room. Filmy sheer curtains with ruffles covered the old wooden window frames, and hand-braided rugs lay on the worn hardwood floors. Alice June had never seen so many handmade things: doilies, needlepointed pillows, crocheted afghans, and best of all, through the open bedroom doors, she glimpsed handmade quilts on each of the beds. Mrs. Lucchetti noticed Alice June's wide eyes and invited her to take a closer look.

"Jacob's Ladder," she said, pointing to a blue and white one with a bold pattern. "And this one is Grandma's Fan." And it did look like a big fan mostly covering large pink squares with yellow sashing.

Mrs. Lucchetti had pictures of her grandkids scattered around, and the tools of her trade: quilting hoops, a sewing machine, baskets of fabric and of knitting.

"Is knitting hard?" asked Alice June.

"Not really," replied Mrs. Lucchetti. "Especially not if you are willing to make mistakes. Would you like a lesson or two?"

Alice June's face lit up brighter than any Christmas tree. "Yes, I would."

"Well, you just come on over next time you're in the neighborhood, and I'll give you one. You may need more than one, and if you do, I'll give you that one, too."

Looking at her mother, Alice June asked, "OK?"

"Sure," said Momma, "If you want to learn, I'll drive you. That's awfully kind of Mrs. Lucchetti. But I'll never figure out where you got your needlework gene."

They all laughed at that, and Alice June thought suddenly of Alice Patricia. Up until now, she hadn't really thought about the fact that, being related, they could have some of the same genes. Or that, maybe, liking to quilt could be genetic.

THEY WENT TO SEE Uncle Bobbie at the end of June, when the days were at their longest, just as the wheat crop was beginning to turn gold in the hills around the tiny town, which nestled in a steep gully. Small, old-fashioned wooden houses of many different hues, with an occasional grand mansion built long ago by some well-off wheat rancher, climbed the sides of Pine Creek's small canyon. Beyond the town, the Blue Mountains rose into the distance, with white fluffy clouds overhead against June's soft sky, marching into the distance as far as you could see.

Alice June had wanted, in one way, to go later, when wheat harvest was on and the rolling hills were deeply golden in every direction, met by brilliant skies of purest turquoise blue, with red combines combing the hills like crawling ladybugs. But Momma's friend in Montana had asked them to come visit her in August, and Alice June would be going to marine science camp in July.

She had been to camp the year before, too, and loved taking walks on the beach every day, writing in a little handmade journal about all the things she had seen that day—sea urchins, jellyfish, bald eagles swooping and soaring, chased by a dozen or more screaming gulls. She had waded knee deep in the warmer, sandy shallows and run from the breakers on the rocky shores. She spent hours treading carefully around tide pools, on the broad shelves of rock at low tide. She slept at night with sand in her sleeping bag from barefoot afternoons, and she slept well.

She loved the salt air, but not any more than she loved the sweet smell of ripe grain, warm in the sun, and the soft, pungent, clean smell of the pine forests that dotted the mountainside above the old homestead. One good thing about going in June was that at home it was still cool and cloudy at that time of year, with all the sea fog, and sometimes it didn't lift all day. At Uncle Bobbie's it would be hot in the daytime and cool at night and sunny every day, and his roses would all be blooming.

It was so different from home, everything about it. The smells, the soft feel of the evening air as it wrapped around you like a warm blanket. Everything was so bustling at home, the breeze sharper with a brisk chill, and here it was so quiet, like a movie that had stopped in the middle, somewhere in the past.

As THEY TURNED OFF the main highway onto a narrow tar road, they traveled over the crest of the hill, and the tiny town dotted with huge old shade trees came into view. Her heart leaped a little higher in her chest. The quilt lay in the trunk, wrapped in paper, inside its enormous shopping bag. She didn't know how or when to give it to him and had wondered about it the whole way over, through the mountain pass where the landscape changed from coastal to desert, at the truck stops, along the windswept Columbia River where huge poplars shielded houses and orchards from the worst of the gusty weather.

He was out in the garden when they pulled up, and his face lit up at the sight of them. He shook her dad's hand warmly, kissed her mother's hand in the old-fashioned way he had and, to Alice June's surprise, he kissed her hand, too, instead of ruffling her hair as he had in the past. It felt funny, but nice. Then he reintroduced them to his roses before they went inside, where the house smelled the same, like Old Spice and beeswax, and the old clock ticked loudly as it always had.

Alice June put her suitcase on a chair in the back bedroom and returned to the grown-ups.

"Is there any place special you'd like to go while you're over here?" Uncle Bobbie was asking.

"I was thinking I'd like to see the old hot springs, the one with the swinging bridge," Alice June's dad said. "Other than that, just strolling around here and smelling the roses sounds like the perfect vacation." And Momma said that just being away from the phone, and having time to read her book, was the perfect vacation for her.

"And you, Alice June?" Uncle Bobbie asked her.

"The hot springs sound nice," she said. But she was thinking of the homestead.

They had only four days to spend and the first two went fast. They went to dinner at the Long Branch, the biggest restaurant in town. There were only two, one being just a soda fountain, and it seemed everyone knew everyone else at the Long Branch, and the food was good, and the portions huge, as though they were all hard-working ranch hands.

Historic pictures hung on the walls and Uncle Bobbie pointed out two that had some of the family in them. There was Uncle Earl on the water wagon and Aunt Kate behind the counter at the hotel. These people were a generation or two older than Uncle Bobbie and were long gone, many years before Alice June was born. But one photograph drew her, suddenly coming into focus. She recognized someone in it.

It was an old group photo, brown with age, of a number of children in paper hats with stars and stripes on them, holding American flags. One face jumped out at her. She called to Uncle Bobbie, who came over and scanned the photo. "Why, it's Alice Patricia. And there's me, and your grandpa. I never noticed this one. It must be the Fourth of July. I don't remember it, but I must have been there," he said and laughed.

She stayed looking at the photo while her mom and dad went on to others. She tugged at Uncle Bobbie's sleeve gently and he bent down to listen.

"Will you take me to the homestead?" she asked.

"Do you mind climbing fences? We might get caught by the owners, if they're there checking on the cattle, you know."

"Would that be bad?"

"The worst they would do is ask us to leave, and they know who I am, after all. I'm willing to risk it if you are."

And so they went, the next morning, she and her great-uncle and her dad. Momma stayed back at the house. The day was going to be hot, and she was immersed in her book.

As they climbed the hill, the early morning birds were still singing, before the heat of the day caught up with them. They helped each other over the barbed-wire fence and the big aluminum stock gate, and as they trudged up the long rutty dirt lane, elderberries and wild roses crowded in on either side of them. Slowly, the curve of the tiny old road led them to a clearing.

A few black cows grazed under the apple trees, which were loaded with green fruit, and tall cottonwoods towered, their leaves rustling, along the banks of the dry creek and over what had been the site of the house. The only sign of people ever having lived there was an old root cellar dug into the side of the hill that rose steeply from the clearing.

Alice June, standing beside Uncle Bobbie, tugged at his sleeve again and asked, in the vast quiet that surrounded them, "Where did Alice Patricia used to sit and sew, mostly?"

Without a word, he led her about 30 feet away and stopped in the shade of two huge old apple trees.

"Here," he said. "The house stood there, and she loved this spot just apart from it. She and Stubby sat here by the hour, on a blanket in the shade, and she sewed. The clothesline was here, and I'd play under it, making forts out of the sheets and blankets," and he laid his hand on a lower branch of the tree and, with surprise in his eyes, picked up his hand again and looked closely at the place it had been. "And here's the old hook that held it." Then he fell silent, and turned his head away.

As the constant breeze blew in their ears, she could hear nothing but its quiet roar and the rustling of the cottonwoods. The creek was dry, as you would expect, even though it was still June. Closing her eyes, she saw a little girl, just her age, bent over her needlework, the wind ruffling her short brown hair that glinted in the sun, her dog asleep next to her. As she opened her eyes, the image lingered in front of Alice June's vision for another second or two, then vanished.

They walked back together without much to say, just listening to the wind and the birds.

CHAPTER TWELVE

AFTER SUPPER THAT NIGHT, Alice June asked her dad for the key to the car's trunk.

"Did you forget something?" he asked with a twinkle in his eye.

"No," she replied, "I remembered something."

Dad went out with her, holding doors open as she brought in the big package, clutched in both arms. Uncle Bobbie was sitting in his favorite chair.

"I brought you something," she said.

"For me?" He sat up straighter. "But it's not my birthday."

"It's for you anyway. Here."

He took the bulky bundle into his lap and slowly, with wonderment on his face, gently removed the tape and paper. As he pulled back the final wrapping to reveal the quilt, his expression changed to a look she could not describe. Curiosity and searching gave way instantly to recognition. His voice was very quiet and it shook as he looked up at her and spoke.

"I remember . . . Alice Patricia . . . she made these squares . . . just before she died. How did you know? Who made these into a quilt? What in the world. . . ."

"I made it," Alice June said. "My quilters' club and me. I thought you should have it."

"But . . . these must have been given to your grandpa. You've worked so hard. It's so pretty. Don't you want to keep it?" He held tight to it and his hands were shaking a little, and his voice was still quiet, almost a whisper.

"I want you to have it. I never knew her. You remember her."

"Oh, but Alice June," his words were tumbling out. "You don't know how much you are like her. Sometimes, when I see you, for a moment I forget she's gone. It's like she never died."

After they had spread it on his bed and he'd heard the whole story and she had convinced him it was really his, he gave her such a hug as she had never had. And, three weeks later, she came home from camp to find a letter.

Dear Alice June,

*I feel 70 years younger after sleeping under your quilt. Sometimes
it seems my sister is back in my room, whispering about something
Stubby did or telling me what she wanted for Christmas and laughing
like she would sometimes do, in spite of all her troubles. She loved
to live, and did it as long as she could, and she put all her heart into
her needlework. I can surely see that now. She was very special, and
very kind. Like I said, you are a lot like her. Thank you, Alice June, for
bringing so much of my sister back home.*

Love,

Uncle Bobbie

It was at a meeting in August that Mrs. Lucchetti asked her if she
was using the quilt yet. Alice June had hesitated to tell them what she had
done with it, thinking they might object to her decision. After all, they had
worked so hard on it, and then she had just given it away. But she wasn't
going to fib about it.

"Well," she said, "Did I ever tell you about Alice Patricia's brother? My
Uncle Bobbie?"

They just looked at her and Betty replied, "I don't believe you did."

"Well," she said again, "He's the only one left who remembers her. He
gave me her sewing box and a lot of other things. He misses her. So," she
said, and swallowed, "I gave it to him."

Every last one of the ladies put down their needles and looked at her.
She looked straight back at them, remembering what Uncle Bobbie had said
about bringing his sister back home. Tears began to gather in her eyes as she
recalled his letter, and she knew she wasn't sorry for what she did. Finally
Mrs. Lucchetti spoke, and beat Betty to it, which was unusual. She said,
simply and quietly, "Good for you, little gal."

Then she picked up her needle and started stitching again, and everyone
else did too. There was important quilting to be done.

Author's Note

Though some of the details changed, this story is essentially true. There was a young girl who lived on a homestead in the beautiful hills of eastern Oregon in the early years of the twentieth century. Her name was Alice Patricia, and she was my aunt. She had two brothers: the littlest one grew up to be my father, and 80 years after his sister's premature death, he still flies the American flag on her birthday to honor her as one of the bravest people he ever knew. She was very ill during the years he knew her, but she lived her life to the fullest and left behind a few photographs; a few whimsical, lovely quilts; and some butterfly squares for us to remember her by. In photos, she strongly resembles my sisters.

I wanted to write this story about her because words have the power to bring people and places to life. I took the stories I'd heard, the photographs I'd seen, and the memories my father shared of this girl, who was very much alive in a different place and time, and tried to bring her back to us the only way I knew how. I have heard it said that if people live in your heart, they are never really gone, and that makes sense to me. Not only does Alice Patricia live in memory, but she also lives through her quilts, which are treasured here in my home and in my heart. Quilts are good that way.

QUILTMAKING INSTRUCTIONS
FOR ALICE'S BUTTERFLIES

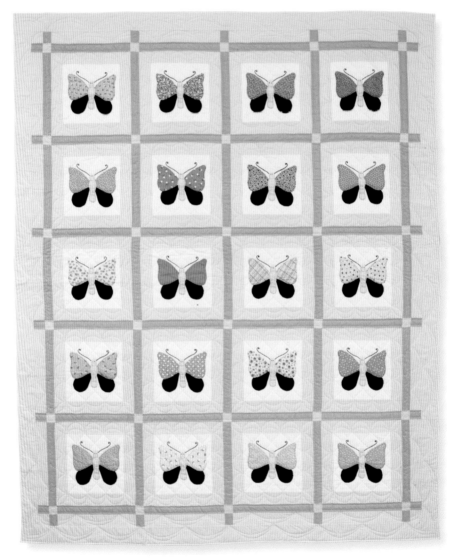

Finished quilt size: 73½" x 89"

Number of blocks: 20 • Finished block size: 14"

MATERIALS

Yardage is based on 42"-wide fabric.

- 5 yards of solid yellow fabric for butterfly bodies, sashing, corner blocks, border, and binding
- 2⅜ yards of solid white fabric for block backgrounds
- 1½ yards of solid lavender fabric for sashing
- ⅝ yard of solid purple fabric for lower butterfly wings
- ¼ yard of solid soft green fabric for cornerstones
- Two 6" x 6" squares *each* of 20 different 1930s vintage reproduction prints for upper butterfly wings
- 6 yards of fabric for backing
- 80" x 95" piece of batting
- Assorted colors of embroidery floss to accent butterfly wings
- 4 skeins of black embroidery floss for butterfly bodies and antennae
- Template plastic or heavy card stock
- Freezer paper
- Embroidery hoop

CUTTING

Prewash all fabrics before cutting. All measurements include ¼" seam allowances.

From the solid white, cut:
- 20 squares, 11" x 11"

From the *lengthwise* grain of the solid yellow, cut:
- 2 strips, 3½" x 160"; set aside for border

The remaining solid yellow fabric will be 35" wide. From this piece, cut:
- 14 strips, 2½" x 35"; cross-cut into 40 rectangles, 2½" x 10½"
- 5 strips, 14½" x 35"; cross-cut into 58 rectangles, 2½" x 14½"
- 4 squares, 2½" x 2½"
- 11 strips, 2½" x 35", for binding

From the solid lavender, cut:

- 3 strips, 14½" x 42"; crosscut into 49 rectangles, 2" x 14½"
- 2 strips, 2" x 42"; crosscut into 22 rectangles, 2" x 2½"

From the solid green, cut:

- 2 strips, 2" x 42"; crosscut into 30 squares, 2" x 2"

CREATING THE BLOCKS

Alice's quilt has hand-appliquéd butterflies embellished with hand embroidery. The instructions that follow are for these techniques. If you prefer a more contemporary look, you can fuse the appliqué and embellish with machine embroidery.

1. Using a permanent marking pen or a pencil, trace the appliqué pattern on page 93 onto the template plastic or heavy card stock. The dashed lines indicate where the appliqué pieces will overlap, and the dotted lines will help in positioning the appliqués on the background. Carefully cut each piece directly on the drawn line.

2. Use the appropriate template to trace 20 lower wings onto the uncoated side of the freezer paper. Flip the template so the wrong side is facing up and trace 20 reversed lower wings. Trace 20 and 20 reversed upper wings and 20 bodies. Cut all these shapes directly on the drawn lines.

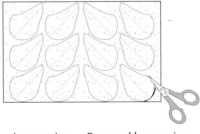

Lower wing.   Reversed lower wing.
Cut 20.   Cut 20.

3. Place the freezer-paper lower wings shiny side down on the wrong side of the purple fabric, leaving ½" between each piece for the seam allowances. Press with a dry iron set on medium heat. The freezer paper will lightly adhere to the fabric.

4. Cut out each piece, adding a scant ¼" seam allowance all around the freezer paper.

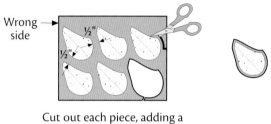

Cut out each piece, adding a
scant ¼" seam allowance.

5. Working from the wrong side of each piece, carefully fold the seam allowance over onto the freezer-paper pattern and hand baste in place. Ease in any fullness for a smooth finished edge. You do not need to turn under the edges of the wings that will be placed under the body and upper wing pieces.

6. Repeat steps 2–5 using an upper wing and a reversed upper wing with matching vintage print squares. Cut a total of 40 vintage fabric upper wings (20 upper wings, each paired with a reversed upper wing in the same fabric). You do not need to turn under the edge of the wing that will be placed under the body. Repeat steps 2–5 with body shapes and the yellow fabric. Turn under all the edges. You will make 20 yellow bodies.

7. Fold the 11" white squares in half, left to right and then top to bottom. Crease gently. Open the squares, fold in half diagonally, and crease

gently. Open the squares, fold in half on the opposite diagonal, and crease gently. The creases will run from corner to corner and through the center.

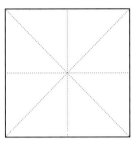

8. Referring to the placement and embroidery guide on page 94, pin a lower wing and a reversed lower wing right sides up on the right side of a white square. Use the crease lines to help position the appliqué. Place the edges of the lower wings 1⅞" from the sides and 2" from the bottom of the background square. Baste in place.

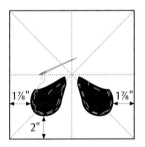

9. Pin an upper wing and a matching reversed upper wing to the square. The edges should be 1¼" from the sides and 2¼" from the top of the square. Baste in place. Don't baste closer than ½" from the underlapping lower wing.

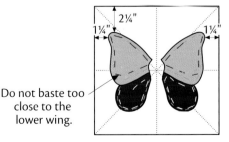

Do not baste too close to the lower wing.

10. Position a body piece on the square, matching the centering lines and overlap lines. Baste in place, keeping the basting stitches at least ½" in from the sides.

11. Repeat steps 8–10 to baste all the appliqué pieces to the remaining white squares.

12. Gently fold back the overlapping body and upper wing from one of the lower wings. Using cotton or silk thread that matches the purple fabric, cut a strand about 18" long, thread it on a needle, and tie a knot at the end. Starting about ⅛" from where the turned-under edge begins, insert the needle into the back of the lower wing piece, bringing it to the front at the edge of the fold.

13. Insert the needle into the background fabric directly under the point where the thread comes to the front. Slide the needle for about ⅛" parallel to the appliqué and bring it to the front, catching just a couple of threads at the edge of the appliqué piece. Don't take too big of a stitch into the appliqué, or you will stitch through the freezer paper.

14. Continue stitching in this manner, gently tugging the thread every few stitches to make it snug but not tight enough to cause distortion. When you reach the end of the turned-under edge, bring the

needle and thread to the back underneath the wing. Take a tiny stitch through just the background fabric and tie one or two small knots. Then run the thread between the background and the wing for an inch or two and cut close to the fabric. The knot will be hidden below the appliqué piece.

15. Remove all basting from the lower wing, and use a pair of tweezers to pull out the freezer paper.

16. Repeat steps 12–15 to appliqué all the lower wings and reversed lower wings to the white squares.

17. In the same manner, appliqué the upper wings to the blocks, and then remove the basting stitches and freezer paper. Appliqué the bodies to the blocks but stop stitching 1" from completion. Remove all basting and use tweezers to carefully pull out the freezer paper. Finish stitching the piece into place. Make 20 blocks.

Make 20.

Adding Embroidery

For best results use an embroidery hoop to keep the work taut.

1. Using the placement and embroidery guide on page 94 as a reference, lightly mark the body and antennae embroidery lines onto the blocks using a pencil or removable marker.

2. Using two strands of embroidery floss in a contrasting color and a running stitch, embroider ⅛" inside the edges of the upper and lower wings. To make a running stitch, bring the needle up from the back at

the beginning of the line to be embroidered. Make small stitches that are evenly spaced and uniform in length.

3. Using two strands of black embroidery floss and a running stitch, embroider the body segments on the butterflies.

4. Using three strands of black embroidery floss, embroider one French knot for each eye. To make a French knot, bring the needle through the fabric from the back to the front in the center of the eye. Wrap the floss firmly around the needle three times and, holding the floss taut, insert the needle as close as possible to the spot where the floss came up from the back. Pull the floss to the back, maintaining an even tension to keep it from getting tangled.

5. Using two strands of black embroidery floss and a stem stitch, embroider the butterfly antennae. End each antenna with a French knot. The stem stitch is worked from left to right, with the floss held either above or below the needle. Bring the needle up from the back at the beginning of the line to be embroidered. Insert the needle about ¼" from this point and bring it back up halfway between. Pull the thread through. On the next stitch, insert the needle ¼" from the first point and bring it up at the end of the previous stitch. Maintaining an even tension, continue in the same manner. This will create a smooth, textured line.

Completing the Blocks

Use a ¼"-wide seam allowance for all seams.

1. Press each block and trim to 10½" x 10½", keeping the butterflies centered. The midline of the butterfly should be 5¼" from the trimmed edges of the block.

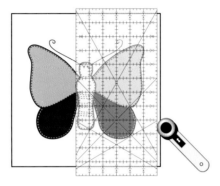

2. With right sides together, stitch the 2½" x 10½" yellow rectangles to the top and bottom of each block as shown. Press the seam allowances toward the yellow.

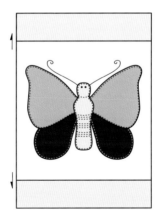

3. With right sides together, stitch the 2½" x 14½" yellow rectangles to the sides of each block as shown. Press the seam allowances toward the yellow.

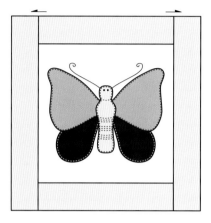

Assembling the Quilt Top

1. To construct a block row, stitch four blocks alternating with five 2" x 14½" lavender rectangles as shown. Stitch one 2½" x 14½" yellow rectangle to each end of the row. Press the seam allowances toward the lavender. Make five block rows.

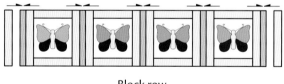

Block row.
Make 5.

2. To construct an inner sashing row, stitch five 2" x 2" green squares alternating with four 2" x 14½" lavender rectangles as shown. Stitch one 2" x 2½" lavender rectangle to each end of the row as shown. Press the seam allowances toward the lavender. Make six inner sashing rows.

Inner sashing row.
Make 6.

3. For the top and bottom sashing rows, stitch five 2" x 2½" lavender rectangles alternating with four 2½" x 14½" yellow rectangles as shown. Stitch one 2½" x 2½" yellow square to each end of the row as shown. Press the seam allowances toward the lavender. Make two rows.

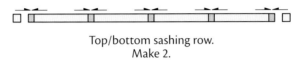

Top/bottom sashing row.
Make 2.

4. With right sides together, join the block rows to the inner sashing rows, matching seams as shown. Press the seam allowances toward the sashing rows. Matching the seams, sew the sashing rows made in step 3 to the top and bottom edges of the quilt top. Press toward the inner sashing rows.

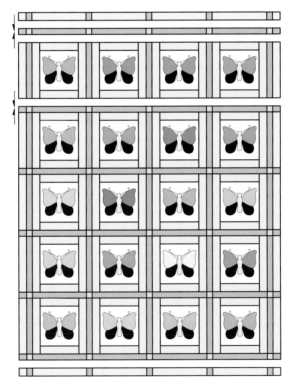

5. Carefully measure the width of the quilt top through the center. Cut one border strip to this length from *each* of the 3½" x 160" strips. Pin the borders to the top and bottom of the quilt top, with right sides together and corners and centers matching, and stitch. Press toward the outer borders.

6. Carefully measure the length of the quilt top from top to bottom, including the borders just added, and cut the remaining two yellow border strips to this length. Pin the borders to the sides of the quilt top, with right sides together and corners and centers matching, and stitch. Press the seam allowances toward the outer borders.

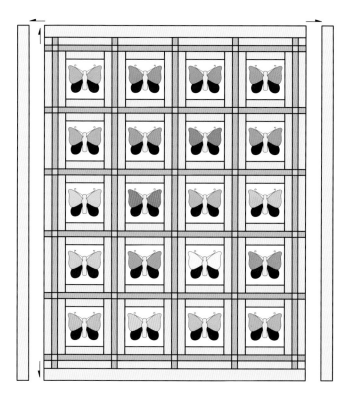

Finishing the Quilt

1. Cut the backing fabric into two 3-yard lengths. With right sides together and a ½" seam allowance, stitch the selvage edges together as shown. Press the seam allowance open.

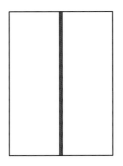

2. Using a removable marking pen or pencil and referring to the diagram below, lightly mark the quilting lines onto the quilt top.

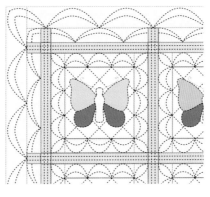

Quilting diagram

3. Working on a large table or the floor, lay out the backing fabric wrong side up and smooth out all wrinkles. Anchor in place with masking tape. Center the batting over the backing, smoothing out any wrinkles toward the outside edges. Center the quilt top over the batting and backing, making sure the batting and backing extend beyond the edges of the quilt top on all sides. Smooth out any wrinkles. Stitch the three layers of the quilt sandwich together using large basting stitches.

Baste lines approximately 3" to 4" apart in horizontal and then vertical rows as shown.

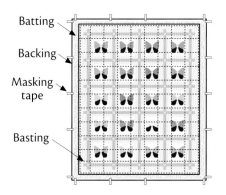

Batting
Backing
Masking tape
Basting

4. Quilt the three layers of the quilt sandwich together following the marked lines. When quilting is complete, trim the excess batting and backing even with the quilt top.

5. Cut the ends of the yellow 2½"-wide binding strips at a 45° angle and stitch the ends together to form one long binding strip. Do not cut the ends of the long binding strip at an angle. Fold the strip in half lengthwise with wrong sides together and press.

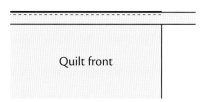

Right side

Fold line

Wrong side

6. Pin the binding to the top edge of the quilt front, aligning the raw edges of the binding with the quilt edge. Stitch the binding to the quilt using a ¼"-wide seam allowance.

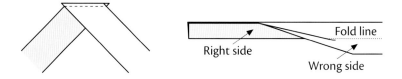

Quilt front

7. Trim the binding even with the end of the quilt. Open the binding away from the quilt so that the folded edge is facing outward. Pin the binding to the second side of the quilt, aligning the raw edges of the binding with the quilt edge. Stitch the binding to the quilt. Repeat for the remaining two sides.

8. Starting at a corner and working from the back, fold the binding edge that has a seam over to the back of the quilt and pin into place. Fold the remaining binding strip to the back and pin. The raw edge on the binding strip will be covered. If you have a raw edge showing, you folded the wrong binding strip down first. Using an invisible hemstitch, sew the binding to the back of the quilt, folding each remaining corner in the same manner.

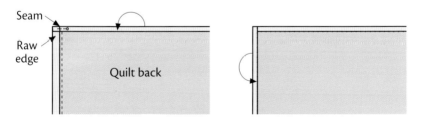

Seam

Raw edge

Quilt back

BUTTERFLY PATTERN

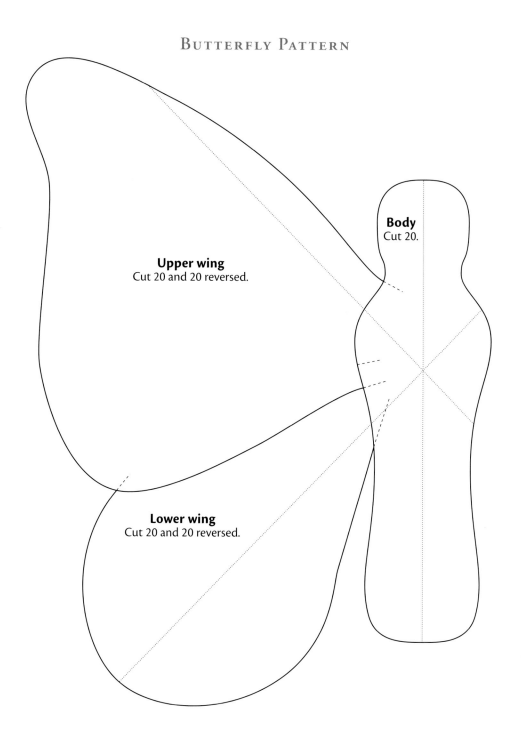

Upper wing
Cut 20 and 20 reversed.

Body
Cut 20.

Lower wing
Cut 20 and 20 reversed.

············· Crease line
— — Running stitch
----- Stem stitch
  ◦ French knot

ABOUT THE AUTHOR

JENNIFER BLOMGREN was born and raised in Forks, Washington. The youngest of three daughters, she spent many of her happiest childhood hours visiting and learning needlework skills from the older ladies of the neighborhood. Her mother taught her to sew, her grandmother taught her to quilt, her father taught her the value of history through books and his own masterful storytelling; and all these gifts have greatly enriched her life.

She works as a registered nurse and in her practice, mostly with the elderly, she finds that the subject of needlework brings her and her patients onto common and familiar ground.

Jennifer's great-aunts in Lynden, Washington, made beautiful quilts using wool from their own sheep, and her step-great-grandmother was a locally famous quilter in the beautiful Blue Mountain foothills of eastern Oregon. The natural beauty of these strikingly contrasting areas, the artistry of handmade quilts, and stories of the lives and times of her relatives has influenced her greatly.

Jennifer has lived almost all her life in the Pacific Northwest, nursing, singing, writing, painting, knitting and sewing, gardening, and appreciating the beauty of the natural world and the love and loyalty of her family and her three beloved dogs. She feels that our modern world in its rush too often leaves behind the things that matter the most: love, connection, patience, quiet, careful attention, and beauty, all of which are exemplified by quilts.